WRITING A LIFE:

L.M. MONTGOMERY

Lucy Maud Montgomery in Leaskdale, Ontario, circa 1916.

Writing a Life

L.M. MONTGOMERY

Mary Rubio
and
Elizabeth Waterston

ECW PRESS

CANADIAN CATALOGUING IN PUBLICATION DATA

Rubio, Mary, 1939–
Writing a life : L.M. Montgomery

Includes bibliographical references and index.
ISBN 1-55022-220-1

1. Montgomery, L.M. (Lucy Maud), 1874–1942 – Biography.
2. Novelists, Canadian (English) – 20th century –
Biography.* I. Waterston, Elizabeth, 1922– . II. Title.

PS8526.045Z89 1995   C813'.52   C94-932054-4
PR9199.2.M6Z89 1995

This book has been published with the assistance of the Ministry of Culture, Tourism and Recreation of the Province of Ontario, through funds provided by the Ontario Publishing Centre, and with the assistance of grants from the Department of Communications, The Canada Council, the Ontario Arts Council, and the Government of Canada through the Canadian Studies and Special Projects Directorate of the Department of the Secretary of State of Canada.

Design and imaging by ECW Type & Art, Oakville, Ontario.
Printed by Kromar Printing, Winnipeg, Manitoba.

Distributed by General Distribution Services,
30 Lesmill Road, Don Mills, Ontario M3B 2T6.
(416) 445-3333, (800) 387-0172 (Canada), FAX (416) 445-5967.

Distributed to the trade in the United States exclusively
by InBook, 140 Commerce Street, P.O. Box 120261,
East Haven, Connecticut, U.S.A. 06512.
Customer service: (800) 243-0138, FAX (800) 334-3892.

Distributed in the United Kingdom by Bailey Distribution,
Learoyd Road, Mountfield Road Ind Est, New Romney, Kent, TW28 8XU.

Published by ECW PRESS,
2120 Queen Street East, Suite 200
Toronto, Ontario M4E 1E2.

ACKNOWLEDGEMENTS

Our greatest debt is to the Social Sciences and Humanities Research Council of Canada for providing funding to the L.M. Montgomery Project through a series of grants. The wide-ranging and interconnected research that has been supported by SSHRCC has produced this book, three volumes of *The Selected Journals of L.M. Montgomery, Kindling Spirit: L.M. Montgomery's* Anne of Green Gables, and *Harvesting Thistles: The Textual Garden of L.M. Montgomery: Essays on Her Journals and Novels*. Still to come are at least one more volume of the journals, and the longer, authorized biography. Without the original encouragement and goodwill of L.M. Montgomery's son, the late Dr. E. Stuart Macdonald of Toronto, and Mrs. Ruth Macdonald, this project would not have been possible. We are also indebted to countless archivists, local historians, librarians, and other researchers in Canadian literature who have all been generous with their time and information. We also thank Nancy Sadek and staff of the University of Guelph Archives and the Office of Research at Guelph who have assisted us in every way possible. Especial thanks also goes to many people on Prince Edward Island — both scholars and relatives of Montgomery. Various scholars in Europe, the United Kingdom, and Scandinavia have provided information that has extended our knowledge of Montgomery's worldwide impact. Finally, we acknowledge the unfailing help and support of Gerald J. Rubio and Douglas Waterston, our husbands.

PHOTOGRAPHS: All of the illustrations in this volume (including the cover and frontispiece) are provided courtesy of the L.M. Montgomery Collection, University of Guelph Archives, except for three: illustration 2 has been provided by John and Jennie Macneill of Cavendish, P.E.I.; illustration 5 is used by permission of the Prince Edward Island Provincial Archives, Charlottetown; illustration 8 is used by permission of George Campbell, Park Corner, P.E.I.

Quotations from L.M. Montgomery's early journals are taken, as indicated in the text, from *The Selected Journals of L.M. Montgomery* (Oxford University Press). All other quotations from the journals are taken from Montgomery's unpublished manuscripts in the L.M. Montgomery Collection in the University of Guelph Archives.

TABLE OF CONTENTS

LIST OF ILLUSTRATIONS

Writing a Life

L.M. MONTGOMERY

INTRODUCTION:
THE STORYTELLER'S GIFT

Every life is a tangled web, a crisscrossing of chance and choice, nature and nurture, free will and fate. Studying the pattern of L.M. Montgomery's life, we can see some obvious threads: her heritage, her position in her family, her era, her birthplace, her schooling, her profession, her marriage, her friends, her foes, her ambition. But weaving through that pattern was an extra strand: the storyteller's gift, the gift of words. In the face of enormous trial, Montgomery held onto that strand. She used it to knot together all of her puzzling experiences, creating memorable, lovable stories with sunny surfaces and darker shadows. Whatever happened to her, whatever she read or heard, she caught in a net of words.

Lucy Maud Montgomery wrote stories and poems from the time she was a child; she began publishing when she was only sixteen. As her life proceeded, she also put her storytelling talents to another use: she trained herself to write up the events of her daily existence in narrative form, entering them in a journal. Writing her secret journal became an exercise in narrative skill, as surely as did composing one of her famous and well-loved "Anne" or "Emily" or "Pat" books. Over an amazingly long stretch of years — 1889 to 1942 — she recorded certain experiences of her life, lingering, hastening, touching up, and playing down. These journals, unpublished in her own time, have brought readers of the last decade a new sense of Montgomery's life, her times, and her attitudes.

Three tensions strained the way Montgomery exercised her storytelling gift. First, she was a woman, at a time when few people questioned the idea that the main job for a woman — even an artistically talented woman — was to get married and raise children. Second, like many women who did insist on writing (in a period when serious writing was considered a male preserve just as getting a good formal education was an option only open to men), she wrote for the popular market, settling for the production of less prestigious but more lucrative wares. Third, her books soon became and long remained best sellers. Their very breadth of appeal roused the scorn of academic critics, who assumed that if a book was a best seller it could not have literary merit, for by definition a mass readership (especially masses of women readers) could not be discriminating in literary taste. But her astonishing success encouraged Montgomery to maintain the tone, style, and themes that had created a world-wide circle of devotees.

Montgomery relished her popularity and worked hard to keep her readers. She also strove to maintain her visible feminine role as charming girl, supportive wife, and sympathetic mother. But she learned to inject subtle ironies into the amiable stories expected of a woman author. She kept her stories light and sparkling, funny and charming, as suited a general and unsophisticated readership, but her books also held their place among best sellers for the adult market because she mixed darker, subtler, and more complex tones into the background of the bright romances.

In a sense Montgomery became a subversive author, building secret messages of rebellion and resistance against authority (especially patriarchal authority) into her sunny stories. No doubt these messages partly explain her enormous popularity among oppressed peoples living in totalitarian regimes.

If her novels contain hidden rebellion, her journals pulse with open resistance, resentment, and depression at the structures of daily life that caught her ambition in cobwebs. She felt trapped in her marriage, confined by motherhood, and bound by the need to present a smiling face of domestic happiness in accord with the romantic novels she was producing. She was fettered by her own popularity and by the need to maintain her success in order to supplement her husband's income as a poorly paid country parson. And she was caught, perhaps unawares, in another trap: her own facility in creating narratives. To keep her secret journal going, she unconsciously adapted her life to her narrative skill. Gradually she began to make life-choices shaped to fit the kind of story she was prepared to tell in that journal.

So Montgomery's gift for storytelling both twisted and reinforced the tangled threads of her life. She never undervalued that gift; it helped her endure considerable trials, which she was then able to convert into amusing anecdotes and engaging plots. For her, writing was a refuge, a solace, and a joy. Luckily, she was able to pass her joy along to others. Whatever the tensions of her life, she never lost the ability to turn her experiences and secret dreams into poignantly memorable fiction. Her words have brought pleasure to many, for through them Montgomery created a circle of friends, a ring of laughter, and a sense of place. And the place, from the beginning, was Prince Edward Island.

A STORY GIRL

Prince Edward Island lies just off the northeastern coast of mainland Canada, curved into the opening breadth of the Gulf of St. Lawrence. On the north shore of the island, a string of small farming communities marks the two-hundred-year adventure in pioneer farming and fishing of Scottish, English, French, and Irish settlers of this smallest of Canada's provinces. In Clifton, Prince Edward Island, a north-shore crossroads hamlet, Lucy Maud Montgomery was born on 30 November 1874. Her mother, Clara Woolner Macneill Montgomery, came from nearby Cavendish village.

When, less than two years later, the pretty 22-year-old mother succumbed to "galloping consumption" (fatal tuberculosis), baby Maud remained in the Cavendish home of Clara's parents, Alexander and Lucy Woolner Macneill. The baby's father, Hugh John Montgomery, agreed. He gave up his Clifton home and his already bankrupt general store, and began a drifting life, gradually shifting westward, like so many young Maritimers, until he finally settled in faraway Prince Albert, Saskatchewan, then part of the Canadian Northwest Territories.

In Cavendish, the baby had joined a large extended clan. Grandmother Lucy Macneill, however, was not a Scot like the rest of the Macneill, Campbell, and Montgomery clans. As a little girl she had come to Canada from Dunwich, on the eastern coast of England. Dunwich had a hauntingly romantic past. In ancient times a major centre of English-continental commerce, its power had eroded with its crumbling shoreline. Huge sections of bluffs had slid into the sea, leaving deep underwater the ancient places of power and worship: legend said that in eleven submerged church towers the bells still rang deep in the sea near Lucy Woolner's home.

Lucy Woolner had grown up and married angular, ironic Alexander Macneill. She had raised a family of six before accepting the new responsibility of little Lucy Maud. Her oldest son was named Leander, after the dashing hero who swam the Greek seas for love of a woman; the second son was straightforwardly named John; the third was Chester, Lucy's brother's name, a name from England, out of key with all the neighbouring Scots. The Macneill daughters, besides Clara who died so young, were Annie and Emily. "What's in a name?" Montgomery would ask many years later in *Magic for Marigold*, a book about a little nameless girl, brought up by her grandmothers after her father, Leander, dies. Like drowned bells deep beneath the sea of consciousness, names from her own childhood would ring in her later novels.

*Maudie's maternal grandparents, Alexander Marquis Macneill
and Lucy Woolner Macneill, in Cavendish, Prince Edward Island.*

The Alexander Macneill home in Cavendish.

Aunt Emily was a young woman of twenty when the baby Maud came into the family. One of Montgomery's earliest memories was of the bustle and excitement of Emily's marriage to a cousin of Hugh John, Montgomery's father.

Sixteen miles to the west along the gulf-shore road, in nearby Park Corner, was another family enclave, home of her Montgomery grandparents. Hugh John was their oldest son; his younger brothers were in the process of finding brides when Montgomery was a little girl. Again many lively entries in her early diary recount the excitement of the young Montgomery uncles' courtships, engagements, and weddings.

Happiness of a different kind reigned across the road from the Montgomery farm. Aunt Annie Macneill Campbell, a wonderful cook and bustling homemaker, lived with kindly Uncle John Campbell and their brood of energetic children — Clara, Stella, George, and Frederica. An elderly great-aunt, Mary Lawson, who visited around in this large family circle, brought each house a budget of gossip, updating one set of cousins on the doings of others, retelling older bits of family history in annually sharpened phrases. Young Montgomery learned to recount Aunt Mary Lawson's best stories, entertaining the Campbell cousins at Park Corner; thirty years later she would incorporate these tales into *The Story Girl* and *The Golden Road*.

Montgomery's principal home in childhood, the Alexander Macneill farmhouse, was also the district post office — a fit distinction for a family that loved to see people and hear and dispense news. Newspapers and magazines flowed through the post office, adding a supplement of provincial, national, and international news to the local budget of gossip and anecdote. As a small child, Maud crouched under the post-office table listening to a shipwrecked sea captain tell of storm and stranding on Cavendish beach. Later she heard her grandfather tell of the wreck of the Marco Polo, fastest clipper ship of its day. Grandfather Macneill spun his tale in a memorable way. Seven years later Montgomery would retell the Marco Polo story as a prize-winning entry in a national essay contest. For the rest of her life, she would weave the same story into public speeches in Ontario.

Thus Montgomery learned her narrative skills from the traditional storytellers, male and female, in her clan. At church — and the Presbyterian church played a dominant role in the life of the Macneill family — she learned other stories, mainly Old Testament accounts of the tribes of Israel, their kings, and their wrathful, powerful God. Memorizing Bible verses and catechisms was enforced; listening to sermons and hearing them analyzed over Sunday dinner was another part of the routine. The cadences of paraphrases of the Psalms of David, the short lines and tight rhyme schemes of old Scottish hymns, all became part of young Maud's inner verbal rhythm. When she wrote her first verses, she echoed these patterns and rhymes.

Other tricks of the trade she learned from her favourite novelists, the authors whose leatherbound books filled the glass-doored bookcases in the Macneill farmhouse: Walter Scott, Charles Dickens, Edward Bulwer-Lytton, W.M. Thackeray, the Brontës. Rhetoric — careful phrasing for maximum effect on the reader or listener — was a staple of her school training. Maud learned to memorize and recite dramatic poems by Macaulay, Scott, Tennyson, Longfellow, Whittier; she was drilled in grammar and spelling; she was encouraged to compose poems, essays, and stories.

Her schoolmates included her cousins, Amanda and Pensie Macneill, destined to remain dear friends throughout her schooldays, plus a tumble of other distant relatives, the Simpsons (less congenial), Mackenzies, Lairds, Clarks, and Stewarts. For awhile there were also two little boys living at the farmhouse: Wellington and Dave Nelson who came "from away" to board with the Macneills, no doubt (like Bev and Felix in *The Story Girl*) serving as audience for Montgomery's first efforts at spinning stories. The schoolchildren shared the excitement when Cavendish community in 1887 built a hall to stage political debates and literary discussions and to house a local library. This lending library provided a wider range of novels and magazines than was

Young Maud Montgomery, aged 14.

*John and Annie Campbell's house in
Park Corner, Prince Edward Island.*

found among the rather traditional fare of Scott and Burns in the Macneill bookcases or on the schoolhouse shelves.

The tiny one-room clapboard schoolhouse was manned (or "womanned") by young teachers from nearby communities, some of them barely older than the bigger pupils. Teaching was the obvious career for a bright, articulate girl such as Maud, and although her grandfather Macneill had an irrational antipathy to female teachers, she could hope to follow in the path of Miss Hattie Gordon, who had been an inspiring and encouraging teacher. Montgomery's Cavendish schoolmate Nate Lockhart could plan to go to Acadia University in preparation for professional life as a lawyer; but whereas Montgomery could flirt with Nate, she could not expect to follow his educational path. At best she could hope to go to teachers college in Charlottetown for a year.

WESTERN TRIP AND
FIRST PUBLICATIONS

First, though, came an unpredictable break in Montgomery's Island childhood. Her grandfather Montgomery was now a member of the Senate of Canada, which met in Ottawa. In 1890, twenty-three years after the confederate British colonies in North America first moved to form the Dominion of Canada, Grandfather Montgomery was very much concerned with the building of branchlines of the railway that already spun westward across the continent, encouraging the old Hudson's Bay Company territories in the northwest to join the Canadian confederation. Grandfather Montgomery planned a trip on the westward-moving railway to visit his wandering son, Hugh John, out in Prince Albert. Hugh John had now remarried, choosing the stepdaughter of a railway magnate, an acquaintance of his father. Senator Montgomery decided to take his fifteen-year-old granddaughter out West with him to meet her new stepmother and perhaps to settle in Saskatchewan.

What new stories would now emerge for a girl already trying her hand at storytelling, poetry, essays, and news articles? Montgomery had kept a sporadic diary since she was a very small child and lately had developed a stronger habit of recording in her journal the doings of her schooldays. Now she was embarking on a nonprovincial life — and her diary could swell to encompass it. She was ready to record and ponder this fabulous transcontinental trip. She was set to pen sharp word-sketches of people out West — her Métis schoolfellows, the frontier townsfolk, the farmers breaking sod on the virgin prairie.

Between August 1890 and August 1891, life in Prince Albert turned up three really good stories — one was infuriating, one funny, one romantic.

Family life with her dear father and petty stepmother was infuriating. Montgomery had longed to join her father. She had also longed for a mother, had felt buffeted at home in Cavendish where jealous aunts and uncles coldly defended their own children's claims against those of motherless (and hence defenceless) Maud. In his new home, her father, a town developer with political ambitions, turned out to be as lovable as ever. But his second wife, Mary Ann, was far from the loving protective mother Maud had yearned for, who found herself turned into a baby-minding drudge, often kept home from school. Montgomery's ambitions were ruthlessly set aside by her young, self-absorbed, and again-pregnant stepmother.

Life in a frontier school had its humorous fringes, however. The young schoolmaster, a religiously inclined fellow from Mary Ann's hometown in Ontario, set out to persuade his sixteen-year-old pupil to marry him. Montgomery's bubbling account in her journal of the unprepossessing courtship of "Mr. Mustard" furnishes a comic antidote to the romantic memories of courting back home in Prince Edward Island.

But romance there was — a tentative boy-girl tenderness stirring between Montgomery and a schoolmate, a gentle, chivalrous redheaded boy named Will Pritchard. Will's sister Laura laughingly encouraged Will's shy romancing.

Maud's paternal grandfather, Senator Donald Montgomery.

Maud's father and stepmother, Hugh John
and Mary Ann Montgomery, circa 1886.

When her first year in Prince Albert was over, Montgomery realized that the western foray had no future, and she returned home, making the 2,500-mile trip back to Prince Edward Island mostly by herself. Her experiences had been on the whole sharp and troubling, but she came back with a diary full of fine reworkings of those experiences. She also came home with a scrapbook containing printed copies of her first published work. There was a poem, "On Cape Leforce," sent home to Charlottetown and published there in November 1890 in *The Daily Patriot*; another poem, "June," also published by the *Patriot*, in June 1891; and "Farewell," published in the Prince Albert *Saskatchewan*. More impressive, there was a prose narrative, "The Wreck of the Marco Polo," submitted to the Montreal *Witness* in an annual competition and printed as a prizewinner there and in a collection entitled *Canadian Prize Stories* in February 1891. Finally, there was an essay on the beauty of Saskatchewan, "A Western Eden," published in June 1891 in the Prince Albert *Times* and reprinted in several other western papers. (All these early works are reprinted in Bolger 28–48.) The story girl was standing at the threshold of adult life, already an accomplished raconteur.

READJUSTMENT AND
TEACHER TRAINING

The first year after her return to Prince Edward Island was a year of disappointment, stagnation — and sociable fun. Grandfather Macneill was unwilling to pay to send the sixteen-year-old Montgomery to Charlottetown for a teachers' training course. Feeling aimless, Montgomery spent part of that winter in Park Corner, nominally to teach piano lessons to her cousins, the Campbell girls — three, five, and seven years younger than herself — and to help Aunt Annie, Uncle John, and young George with work in the house and on the farm. The Campbell home would generate one of her major themes: the joy of being part of a secure, laughing family.

The cousins were still at school in Park Corner, but their social life included Montgomery, and her weekends were filled with parties, picnics, church socials, and sleigh rides with a happy crowd of local boys, the Howatts, Stewarts, and McLeods.

Part of this same winter she spent with her aunt Emily Macneill Montgomery at Malpeque, farther west along the north shore of the island. Part of the course was spent at home with increasingly irritable grandparents. These elderly people were far from keen on having Montgomery's young friends and cousins drop in to visit her when she was in Cavendish. Her diary alludes to battles of will with her sharp-tongued grandfather.

The end of this year of marking time, however, saw Montgomery's grandmother and father putting together enough money to send her off to Prince of Wales College in Charlottetown. She went back to Cavendish for a final year to prepare for entrance examinations. With one of her classmates, redheaded Austin Laird, she sparred and exchanged insults, teasing him about his auburn hair, a situation she would invert much later when she wrote *Anne of Green Gables*. She studied hard for the provincial matriculation examinations and placed fifth in the province.

There were 176 young people at Prince of Wales College, mostly boys and girls from farm communities on the island. Montgomery experienced the fun — and the mishaps — of a teenager away from home for the first time. She boarded at an adventure-filled house, sharing a room with her third cousin, Mary Campbell. She strengthened ties of kinship with her Charlottetown first cousins on the Montgomery side, the McIntyres. Social life revolved around the big Zion Presbyterian church, though her interest in church services fluctuated according to the comings and goings of her cousins, the Sutherland boys. Intellectual life at Prince of Wales College was sharpened in debating societies and the college newspaper, and it deepened in traditional courses on everything from English literature to modern farm practices (the latter of major importance to would-be rural teachers).

Maud Montgomery, aged 16.

Montgomery's contributions to the college paper, the *Record*, are good undergraduate humour. Her favourite professor encouraged her to pursue her literary ambitions. She did very well in her final exams and had the honour of reading an essay on Shakespeare's Portia at the spring commencement exercises — a good essay reprinted and praised in the Charlottetown *Guardian*.

Now, however, she had to set aside literary ambitions and concentrate on finding a paying job as a school teacher. Montgomery had crowded a two-year curriculum at Prince of Wales College into a single year in order to get wage-earning work as soon as possible. Finding a teaching position was not easy. Most aspiring teachers were driven by their parents or brothers to outlying schools for interviews. Montgomery's applications got no such encouragement from her grandfather; she could only apply to nearby schools or ones that were walking distance from train stations. Finally, in the late summer of 1894, she found a suitable situation in Bideford for the coming school year.

Bideford, 66 miles west of Cavendish on the far side of Malpeque Bay, was still a bustling town, prosperous from a long-established ship-building enterprise. The students were bright and well motivated; the young people of the neighbourhood were welcoming. One young man named Lou Dystant became a steady companion at church socials and other Bideford events. Warmed by the friendly atmosphere, comfortable in her boarding situation in the home of the Methodist minister, Montgomery pulled out her writing materials and went to work in earnest. Early in the mornings before school began, she would write and revise poems and stories, send them off in a businesslike manner to Canadian and American magazines, revise the rejected submissions, and glory in the accepted ones — a poem in the Toronto *Ladies' Journal* and a story, "A Baking of Gingersnaps," published in the same journal in July 1895. She signed this and other stories in her twentieth year "Maud Cavendish."

Enough money rewarded her efforts that she could plan a year of university in spite of her grandfather's disapproval. Her grandmother offered to cover half the cost of a year at Dalhousie University, in Halifax, Nova Scotia. Montgomery resigned from Bideford school at the end of June, and spent the summer at home, writing — except for a long interval when Uncle Leander brought his wife and family home for a visit and everything except cooking and housekeeping had to be suspended.

Autumn came, and like many young Island men — and a very few Island women — Montgomery prepared to go to university. There was no university on Prince Edward Island, but Dalhousie had long welcomed Islanders. Montgomery moved into Halifax Ladies' College, a residence dominated by clever but daunting female academics. The young Islander quickly found a niche in the Dalhousie *College Observer* and in the university literary society, the Philomathic. She presented papers on contemporary novelists; published and won prize money for her publications in the Halifax *Evening Mail*; wrote major assignments on Milton and Carlyle; and contributed sprightly pieces to the Halifax *Herald*.

Montgomery struggled with poor health that year, coming down with colds, measles, and flu and losing several weeks of schooling. Sometimes she would make forays into the city to visit acquaintances such as the Dystant family, relatives of her Bideford friend Lou, but she formed no permanent friendships with university classmates.

The ending of the year coincided, sadly, with the end of Montgomery's educational career: her money had run out. She had had surprising success, however, in selling short stories and poems to paying magazines: *Golden Days* of Philadelphia, *Youth's Companion* of Boston, McClure's *Chicago Inter Ocean*. But there was no glorious award or scholarship to supplement this success and make further university studies possible. No support for a promising young scholar was forthcoming from her grandparents or such prosperous relatives as Uncle Leander, now entrenched in a major church job in New Brunswick.

According to her later journal entries, Montgomery bitterly resented this lack of support. At the time, however, she recorded no major effort on her own part to enlist assistance. Perhaps she knew that such enterprise would be hopeless, given her grandfather's antipathy. Perhaps she could not face bucking the community's expectations of "ladylike" behaviour. Certainly the pull of college was countered by another very strong urge: the desire to return home to the Island. For despite all the frustrations she experienced in her home life, Montgomery was subject to overwhelming homesickness whenever she was away from the Macneill homestead. Her own room, the village life, and above all her nearness to the seashore and access to the unique beauty of Island hills and fields and woods — these constituted the pull of home.

ENGAGEMENT TO EDWIN SIMPSON

Montgomery returned home, but in the summer of 1896 again faced the difficulty of getting to interviews in order to secure a teaching job. This time her problem was solved by another third cousin, Edwin Simpson. Planning for a career as a minister, Ed had been teaching at his home school in Belmont in order to make enough money to pay his way through college. Now he was ready to complete his theological studies before entering the Baptist ministry. He would arrange for Montgomery to take over his place in the Belmont school and would also find a boarding-house for her: she would board with the Frasers, do her writing there, and spend her weekends with Ed's family in Belmont. Ed would, in short, organize her life. And before the year at Belmont was over, he would propose to his vivacious cousin, in obvious expectation that she would be delighted to become the wife of a minister.

Montgomery accepted Ed's proposal without delight. During that year in the uncongenial little village of Belmont she had become so unhappy that she suffered a bout of deep depression. Her journal entries became flat and tired, sparkling only when she turned with sardonic realism to the strange behaviour of Ed's

"My own dear den": Maud Montgomery's bedroom in her grandparents' Cavendish home.

The Reverend Edwin Simpson, circa 1905.

brothers or to the coarse and uncouth life in her boardinghouse or in the homes of her commonplace pupils. In the spring of that year she heard with shock and grief that her cheery Prince Albert comrade, Will Pritchard, had died of influenza and its complications. Her agreement to marry Ed Simpson, then, came in a period of discouragement when it appeared she had no future other than the gruelling life of a country schoolmarm destined to live in other people's uncomfortable houses.

The following school year, 1897–98, Ed, according to plan, went back to college after helping Montgomery find a teaching position elsewhere. "Elsewhere" turned out to be a village on the south shore of Prince Edward Island, the small town of Lower Bedeque. This time she boarded with a prosperous farm family, the Leards. Montgomery spent a strange year in the Leard home. The family had a son, Herman, an attractive, highly regarded young man with whom she fell deeply in love. Yet she was still engaged to Ed Simpson, whose letters and visits were increasingly disturbing to her. Montgomery realized that she must break the engagement, regardless of her new growing passion for Herman. Ed, however, sublimely refused to believe that anyone could not want to marry him: he rejected her rejection out of hand.

WRITING UP HER LOVE-STORY

The story of this double dose of suitors is important for two reasons. First, at that time the choice of a mate would fully determine any woman's future. If Maud accepted Edwin Simpson as a husband, she would probably have to leave Prince Edward Island; if she chose Herman, she would remain on an Island farm. Ed confidently looked forward to a distinguished career and to powerful influence over his parishioners; Herman, at twenty-six, was permanently settled into the small Lower Bedeque community. Physical contact with Ed left her cold and distressed; Herman's kisses triggered a flooding, passionate response. But in the future, she knew, Ed's sharp — often too sharp — intellect would stimulate, arouse, and irritate her into intellectual response, while Herman's educational limitations would perhaps curtail her chances of mental and aesthetic growth. The choice would be a binding one: there was no divorce on the Island, and no chance, once married, of resisting the dominance of either minister or farmer.

The second reason why this was a crucial situation is that courtship stories dominated popular fiction at this time. As a female writer, L.M. Montgomery would be constrained to focus on love and romance as central topics if she hoped to sell her fiction, particularly if she hoped to create stories that would satisfy adult women readers. Charlotte Brontë and George Eliot (Mary Ann Evans) were her lifelong models: both had focused their novels on the trials of women shaken by passionate sexual love yet torn by other desires — sense of duty, conformity to prudence, dreams of independence and benevolence. Montgomery's personal experience of this common feminine dilemma would add to the vicarious experiences gained through reading, and it might enrich and deepen her fiction.

All this time the basic passion of Montgomery's life — her enduring commitment to a writing career — was keeping pace with the development of her new passion for Herman and the withering of her previous engagement to Edwin. Between stormy sessions of wooing, she wrote, and she mailed, and she published. While some of her story titles reflect her focus on education — "The Prize in Elocution" and "The Extra French Examination" (both published in the spring of 1898 in the *Philadelphia Times*) — others point to her romantic difficulties: "Which Dear Charmer?" "A Strayed Allegiance," "Courage for the Occasion," "Her Pretty Golden Hair," and "Kismet." The tone of these courtship stories, given the agony of indecision Montgomery was herself undergoing, is astonishingly light. She was fitting her fiction to the market rather than drawing it from her own emotional depths. Still others of the year's titles preview themes and motifs to be developed six or seven years later, when

Montgomery as "country schoolmarm."

Montgomery began writing the "Anne" books. One of these, "Miss Marietta's Jersey," published first in *Household* in July of this stressful year, would become part of a chapter of *Anne of Avonlea*, published as a novel ten years later. Montgomery's skill in creating lively, engaging characters and involving them in humorous, suspenseful situations remained strong, even when she was torn by stress and indecision in her personal life.

Besides the outpouring of fictional stories, Montgomery was also developing an addictive habit of writing in her diary. In the journal pages she turned the raw materials of her life into a life-*story*, a continuous narrative written for a private audience of one — herself. She drew events from her own life, selectively, carefully, and artistically, reshaping them in the light of the books she had been reading. In Olive Schreiner's *The Story of an African Farm* she found a fearless, iconoclastic, and speculative heroine, while Charlotte Brontë's *Jane Eyre* presented a woman trying to maintain her selfhood in spite of domineering males and dominating passions.

Increasingly Montgomery selected and wrote up incidents that accorded with the models found in these empowering books; eventually she began to shape her life by making choices that fitted the pattern emerging in the journal. Her writerly power was taking over the direction of her life. Thus the story of the two suitors, Ed and Herman, true in emotional tenor, became infused with a narrative dynamic of its own. Like the heroines of Schreiner and Brontë, Montgomery pictured herself to be threatened by the men who loved her but resented her literary ambitions. Never a public firebrand, the Montgomery of the journals burns with indignation, resistance, and self-definition. But her instinct for literary shaping finally had a curious effect on her journals. For us they appear the "true" revelation of a hidden life; but behind them no doubt a further life is hidden — the part of life not selected for diary entries, the part that was too banal or unfit to be entered into the journal without reshaping and intensifying. Montgomery's account of her passion for Herman Leard, fascinating in itself, becomes

L.M. Montgomery in 1898.

doubly so in the light of our dawning recognition of how much reshaping the journal underwent.

INTERRUPTIONS

In "real" life, threads of conflict tightened, and then were suddenly cut. In March a message from Cavendish brought shocking news: Montgomery's grandfather, Alexander Macneill, had died suddenly; she was bound to return home to help her grandmother straighten out affairs on the farm. These affairs centred on the fact that Grandfather Macneill had left his house and farm to John F. Macneill, the son who had stayed next door and built up a good farm enterprise of his own. The old family house, of course, would be grandmother's to live in — but only as long as she could maintain it. Her son, anxious to claim it along with the farm buildings, was therefore reluctant to give his mother much assistance.

Because Grandmother Macneill was too old to live in the house alone, Montgomery's funeral-visit home was followed by a permanent return. She finished her teaching term in Lower Bedeque and resettled in Cavendish. Yet Uncle John's bad temper and her dependent grandmother's unhappiness began to wear her down. She also experienced sporadic interference with her writing regime since she now had to perform the role of assistant postmistress, old Mrs. Macneill having become nominal postmistress in the Macneill home.

Montgomery, who had come back to the Island with at least half-hearted hopes of one day returning to the mainland to complete her education, now found herself bound to an even smaller sphere. The small farm, the post office, the path to the seashore, the lane to the church — these formed her perimeter now. Yet in her journal she wrote that she was growing more and more engrossed in her writing: "Nearly everything I think or do or say is subordinated to a desire to improve in my work" (1: 228).

Within a year came news that one possible escape route from her lonely isolation was closed: young Herman Leard had been stricken by illness in June 1899 and had died, deeply mourned by his community, at the age of twenty-eight. Montgomery had said goodbye to him a year earlier in the heat of her passion. Now, with pangs of grief, she lived over again "all those mad sweet hours and those sad bitter hours" (*Selected Journals* 1: 240–41).

Another older, more deeply meaningful link to the outer world was to be cut in the next year. Hugh John Montgomery, her beloved father, died out West early in 1900. For a few dark weeks even her ambition seemed dead — she could not rouse herself to pick up her pen. Yet, facing the world alone, Montgomery knew that her only equipment was her "knack of scribbling." In her diary she questioned the value of this knack: "Is it a feather's weight — or is it a talent of gold that will eventually weigh down the balance in my favor?" (1: 249).

PROGRESS AS A WRITER

Montgomery's future seemed precarious. Hugh John had left his daughter two hundred dollars in his will; she had earned another hundred over the course of the year from her stories and poems. This was hardly enough to guarantee even a meagre living. Yet her sales were growing again, some of them to better-known magazines such as *Good Housekeeping* and *Munsey's*. Of the eleven stories published in 1900, six were picked up and reprinted by magazines other than the first publisher, creating a welcome doubling or tripling of income from each story.

The content of the stories was thin: light courtship with trick endings. The following year's stories included such titles as "Lilian's Roses," "Miriam's Lover," "The Courtship of Josephine," "The Waking of Helen," and "The Setness of Theodosia" — all redolent of formula romance. But the tales are well managed, and each has some redeeming touch of whimsy. Confident in her knack, her gift of words, Montgomery pressed on, even in the depressing isolation and stagnation of the Cavendish household in winter.

Then, in September 1901, Montgomery was offered a temporary job as substitute proofreader for the Halifax *Morning Chronicle* and *Daily Echo*. Uncle John's son agreed to live with Grandmother Macneill for the winter. Yet after the job ended, Montgomery seems to have made little effort to find other employment in Halifax. Still, the interlude had been invigorating. Her journal entries acquired a fresh sparkle around this time, and her story writing doubled.

Twenty-five of Montgomery's short stories appeared in a wide range of domestic, church, and farm magazines in 1902. The following year she sold two serial stories. Moreover, Montgomery was now beginning to write stories that would continue to please her, stories she would choose to incorporate into her book-length works over the next few years. "A Pioneer Wooing," for example, the story of her ancestress Betty Sherman, appeared in *Farm and Fireside* in September 1903, was reprinted in *Canadian Courier*, and eventually appeared in *The Story Girl* in 1911. "Polly Patterson's Autograph Square," from *Zion's Herald* in 1904, reappeared, slightly altered, in chapter 23 of *The Golden Road* in 1913.

The severe Island winters were times of depression for the lonely young Montgomery. She did, however, make two lifelong female friends during this period. The carefree companionship of Nora Lefurgey and the stronger, deeper tie with her cousin Frederica (Frede) Campbell lifted Montgomery's spirits at this time.

ENGAGEMENT TO EWAN MACDONALD

In the spring of 1903, something happened that would shift the pattern of Cavendish life. A new minister was inducted in the Presbyterian church. The Reverend Ewan Macdonald was thirty-three years old, unmarried, good-looking, and cheerful. Since Montgomery was church organist as well as village postmistress, she and the minister met frequently — on church committees,

The Reverend Ewan Macdonald, circa 1906.

at supper parties, choir practice, and once at a wedding where he officiated and she was bridesmaid.

Ewan Macdonald came from the eastern part of Prince Edward Island. Like Montgomery, he had attended Prince of Wales College and Dalhousie University; then he had gone to the Presbyterian theological college in Pine Hill, Nova Scotia. Of his farming family, one brother was a doctor, two had gone West, and a fourth brother was prepared to stay on the farm; Ewan, like the younger son of many a Scottish family, was the boy destined for the ministry. When he was inducted into the Cavendish church in September 1903, two ministers participated in the service: one, the Reverend Edwin Simpson, had already played a significant part in Montgomery's past; the other, the Reverend Edwin Smith, would fill a role in her life in the future.

Ed Simpson was still paying the occasional call that September, still quoting poetry: "*thou* / Beside me singing in the wilderness, / O, wilderness were Paradise enow" (*Selected Journals* 1: 289). Before long, however, he left for Chicago to become pastor of a city church.

In the spring of 1905 Ewan Macdonald came to board at John Laird's, close to the Macneill farm. By the autumn of 1906, he had proposed marriage, and been accepted. Both proposal and acceptance had been hastened by the fact that he had decided to leave Cavendish and go to the University of Glasgow in Scotland for graduate studies in divinity.

Soon after recording the engagement in her journal, Montgomery noted that she had just sold one of her best short stories, "The Quarantine at Alexander Abraham's," to *Everybody's* magazine for a hundred dollars. "*Everybody's* is one of the big magazines," she added, "and to appear in it is a sign that you are getting somewhere" (1: 325). "The Quarantine" is a rollicking, good-humoured story about a middle-aged spinster and bachelor, both fiercely opinionated, but both in the end acceding to the desire for comfort and companionship in marriage. Montgomery concluded her journal entry about this farcical romance with a reminiscence about her love for Herman Leard: "[T]hat

The Reverend Edwin Smith, circa 1903.

old love, that old temptation, that old anguish. It stirred my soul to depths that I would never otherwise have sounded . . ." (1: 325). There are no passages like this concerning Ewan, nor is there a running account of their relationship similar to the earlier happy tales of flirtation with Lem McLeod, Jack Sutherland, Lou Dystant, and the other lads of her youth.

ANNE OF GREEN GABLES

During her secret engagement to Ewan, Montgomery continued to live in relative isolation with her grandmother. The years between 1900 and 1908 were lonely but productive ones. Every day she would find time for a long walk along the farm lane, across to the old schoolhouse, down the ferny stretch of "Lover's Lane" toward the Cavendish road, then through farm fields toward the seashore. As she walked along, fitting her pace to the seasonal rhythms of nature, Montgomery would listen to inner voices engaged in imaginary dialogues, voices teasing or taunting, slyly cajoling or humbly pleading. Then she would return home to write at the kitchen table or at the small desk in her bedroom, composing the stories that had been phrasing themselves in her mind.

Out, then, would go the stories, mailed secretly from the Cavendish post office (maintained in the selfsame kitchen); some still came back with rejection slips, but a growing number made it into print. Published in the myriad magazines flourishing to feed the hunger for light fiction, schoolday tales, love stories, courtship stories, tales of gothic terror in dark and ghostly settings, Montgomery's early stories shine with her own deft touches of description, dialogue, and plot. Essentially, they deal with the lives of girls and women "akin to Anne," and are being reissued in collections edited by Rea Wilmshurst.

Montgomery's most vivid journal entries at this time describe the books she was reading in the intervals between housekeeping and turning out short stories. One book in particular made a deep impression: in Elizabeth von Arnim's *Elizabeth and her German Garden* she found the story of a woman's lonely search for autonomy and self-expression. At intervals, too, Montgomery reread her early journals, using them as reassurance of her own vitality. Lingering over her journals, she kept a fresh sense of what her girlhood had been like.

What the 1905 diary does not record is that she was now working on the manuscript of a full-length novel, the book that would become *Anne of Green Gables*. Ewan's courtship had cast a rainbow light of hope. Montgomery could now dream of escape from the dreary life of a Cavendish spinster. With the arrival of a suitable, enviable suitor, she found her spirits rising. Now she could find the courage to spin a full-length tale about the coming of an unwanted child into an oppressive house and community, the tale of that child's conversion of repressive Green Gables into a happy home.

In that summer of 1905, for the first time, Uncle Leander did not bring his large family to visit (and to be fed, entertained, conversed with, and ministered to by his housekeeping niece). That summer, the summer of writing *Anne of Green Gables*, Montgomery could note in her diary: "I write and read and ramble and dream and revel in my garden — and life is so pleasant and peaceful that it actually frightens me" (1: 307). After she had accepted Ewan and he had gone away to Scotland, the journal reverted back to its darker tones. Montgomery was still writing with vigour and variety, however, and in 1907 she produced another full-length serial story, "Una of the Garden," which she would later revise into *Kilmeny of the Orchard*. This love story, told from the point of view of a man coming to Prince Edward Island from Nova Scotia, hinges on the power of love to release a lost voice in a beautiful, artistic woman.

Letters from Ewan revealed the fact that he, too, was experiencing a dark period. He had suffered earlier depressions in his teens and again when away at college in Halifax. Now, in Glasgow in the winter of 1906–07, he was overcome with depression and insomnia. In April 1907 he came home to Canada and accepted a charge in a village at the western end of Prince

FICTION

L. M. Montgomery—a face of balance and refinement. The smooth high
forehead shows love of stories and sympathetic perception, the height and
squareness above the temples and the
arched eyebrows suggest poetic feeling
and artistic taste, while the full eyes
show facility of expression.

"Getting somewhere."

Edward Island, too far for anything but brief and rare visits back to Cavendish.

But April brought a rejuvenation of Montgomery's spirits. The manuscript of *Anne*, which had been circulating rather sadly among publishers, had found a home. On 15 April came a letter of acceptance from the L.C. Page Company of Boston. Page not only accepted *Anne of Green Gables* — they asked for a sequel.

Anne of Green Gables came onto the book market at a propitious time: increasing literacy worldwide had created a huge readership of men, women, and children ready to devour popular fiction with good plots and strong characters. Early in the twentieth century a series of major books had appeared, including such works as Rudyard Kipling's *Kim* (1901) and Kate Douglas Wiggin's *Rebecca of Sunnybrook Farm* (1903), which presented spirited children striking out into the world on their own. Foreshadowed by Louisa May Alcott's *Little Women* (1868) and Mark Twain's *The Adventures of Huckleberry Finn* (1884), these books marked a shift from Victorian attitudes towards childhood. Their child protagonists made them particularly suitable for children, but all were read and relished by adults as well. Eventually *Anne of Green Gables* would take its place among these enduring classics.

Montgomery's novel traces the development of a young girl, volatile and extravagant in speech and action, from a disruptive childhood to a dignified young adulthood. As Anne grows up, her home and social world mellow. Throughout the novel two other strands develop: Anne's warm devotion to Diana, her "kindred spirit," and her stubborn resistance to Gilbert, her clever, hard-working admirer and rival. The story of Anne's recurrent "scrapes" — getting Diana drunk, dyeing her red hair green, nearly drowning in a poetic excursion — is set against a poignant natural setting. Against the recurring seasons of Prince Edward Island, Montgomery poses the uniqueness of human growth — a changing body, a developing mind, new roles, new relationships — as Anne moves with candour and courage toward the "bend in the road" that will mark her maturing.

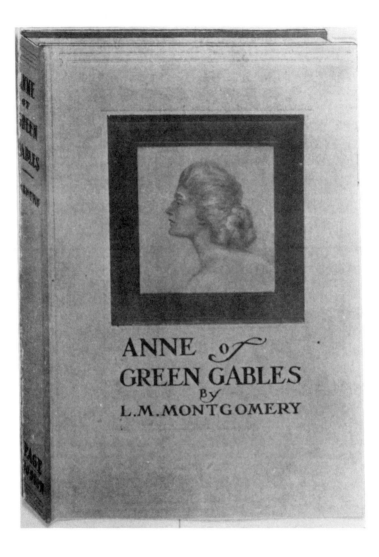

The cover of the 1908 Anne of Green Gables.

A SEQUEL: *ANNE OF AVONLEA*

The springtime mood of exhilaration, initiated when Montgomery received news that *Anne of Green Gables* had been accepted, soon dissolved into letdown. By the end of 1907 she was recording a feeling of "great and awful *weariness* . . . coupled with a heavy dread of the future — *any* future. . . . [T]o be happy would require more effort, more buoyancy, than I shall possess" (*Selected Journals* 1: 333). She was in the trough of a deep cycle of depression, yet in spite of this, she worked on a new book throughout the dark winter, pausing to welcome the first copies of *Anne of Green Gables* in June. On 3 August 1908, Montgomery was rejoicing again: "Today I finished my second book" (1: 338).

Anne of Avonlea follows Anne into her year of teaching, in a school very much like the ones Montgomery herself attended and taught in. The story, with its emphasis on the persuasion and encouragement of individual students, reflects Montgomery's avid reading of modern educational theorists. Anne is also "of Avonlea" in her leadership of a movement to beautify the village, another obsession of this first decade of the twentieth century. But the main story concerns the twins, Davy and Dora. Here Montgomery identifies with the naughty, free-wheeling Davy, expressing her dissatisfaction with dutiful domesticity in her treatment of the good, timid Dora.

She complicates this male-female polarization by introducing a famous woman novelist who moves freely through Avonlea. Anne is at first comically overprepared for this woman's visit, and she doesn't come; later, when the novelist appears, Anne is farcically underprepared. But this reflection of the new power of woman as artist is subordinated to the old one of woman as object of romantic courtship. Although the romance of Anne and Gilbert is still suspended, a romantic marriage is provided for Miss Lavendar, an "old maid" who has been marginalized in Avonlea.

Anne of Avonlea also contains a story within a story — a metafiction (or fiction about fiction) in the form of a garden idyll composed by Anne. She characterizes her idyll in terms that could apply to the whole novel: "There is no *plot* in it. . . . It's just a string of fancies. . . . [E]ditors insist on plots . . ." (158–59). Editors notwithstanding, readers loved the new novel in spite of its refusal to provide the expected romantic closure: Anne remains unmarried at the end of the book.

This sequel to *Anne of Green Gables* reflects some of Montgomery's new sentiments in 1908: her resentment of gender-enforced roles, her romantic dreams, her growing sense of the power and destiny of a person gifted with a flair for writing. Her horizons were broadening. She was now receiving ever-greater batches of fan mail, letters not only from people she had known, but also from hundreds of readers unknown to her. A letter of congratulation from Mark Twain stirred joy and awe.

Nevertheless, Montgomery was lonely. She felt she had exorcised the distressing memory of Ed Simpson's courtship after he returned with an American bride to Cavendish for a brief visit. News of the death of her unpleasant stepmother revived old memories from the West, increasing her loneliness. There was little invigorating innovation in life in Cavendish; the most energetic of her contemporaries had left for greater opportunity on the mainland. Montgomery's only release came through her always inventive imagination.

WRITING *THE STORY GIRL*

Montgomery was already working on a new book, *The Story Girl*. But her rate of production was too slow for her publishers: they urged her to interrupt the new work and quickly revise for publication a serial tale earlier published as "Una of the Garden." She finished this off as *Kilmeny of the Orchard* late in 1909, mailed it to Page in Boston in January 1910, and returned to work on *The Story Girl*. Not surprisingly, this spasm of composition was followed by a descent into deep depression — what she called "nervous prostration — an utter breakdown of body, soul, and spirit" (*Selected Journals* 1: 392).

The monetary rewards for her novels had been enormous. In 1910 she received royalty payments totalling $7,000 — at that time the average Island worker's annual income was less than $300. But her old grandmother discouraged her from spending anything on increasing the comfort of the cold, draughty Macneill farmhouse. Indeed, the fact that the house was to revert to Uncle John Macneill as soon as her grandmother died made expenditures seem foolish, and he was not willing to contribute to its upkeep while they were still in it. Montgomery groaned at the prohibitions: of comfort, of travel, of entertainment, of household help.

Her current book, *The Story Girl*, looked back to a warmer world. In it, a happy crowd of cousins fill an old family farmhouse with laughter, pranks, and harmless flirtations. The fascinating centre of this circle is Sara Stanley, the gifted girl who holds the group spellbound by her stories. Montgomery happily contrasts the Story Girl's charm with the more obvious prettiness of cousin Felicity, the timid gentleness of Cecily, the matter-of-factness of Dan, the gaucheries of Peter the hired boy, and the bewildered insecurity of the cousins from Toronto who tell this Island story. With this book the "story-girl" author was vicariously experiencing the very rewards she herself longed for: audience response, affection, and the glory of feeling one's craft put to best effect.

A recurring theme of the Story Girl's tales is the confrontation of problems of faith, sin, morality, judgement, and the afterlife. The whimsical treatment of preachers and dogma masks the torturing doubts of Montgomery as she contemplated her future as a woman engaged to a Presbyterian minister, knowing that her own faith was very shaky indeed. She had seriously discussed these theological teasers in correspondence with two old pen-pals, Ephraim Weber of Alberta and George Macmillan of Scotland.

The Story Girl was finished in October 1910. Anticipating its success, the publisher, L.C. Page, invited Montgomery to visit him in Boston. While she was a rather uncomfortable and awed visitor in his house, he pressured her to sign a five-year contract, binding her to give him any work she produced in that period. She signed, although she was already disturbed by rumours about Page's methods, which had been hinted at by his disgruntled Canadian agents in the Musson Book Company of Toronto. The Boston visit sealed her uneasiness about Page, but *The Story Girl* was already launched and on its way to the best-seller lists.

In the fall of 1910, Montgomery garnered another reward. She had been invited to meet the Honorable Earl Grey, Governor General of Canada, on his official visit to Prince Edward Island. The public recognition was very welcome. Although fan letters arrived daily by the hundreds, these had less power to free the author from the "ceaseless tyranny in petty things" at home (*Selected Journals* 2: 17).

Ewan Macdonald was now far away. He had accepted a Presbyterian charge in central Ontario, ministering to the two churches of Leaskdale and Zephyr. Marriage was still only a dim possibility as long as Grandmother Macneill lived on. When *Kilmeny* — that story of love releasing a repressed artist — appeared in May 1910, Montgomery noted disingenuously in her diary: "*Kilmeny* reflects very little out of my own experience" (2: 45).

NEW ENDEAVOURS

In January 1911, Montgomery's journal records a new enterprise. At her publisher's urging, she was looking over the mass of short stories produced in recent years, choosing a few that could be revised and tied to the character of Anne — a relatively easy way to produce a new "Anne" book for the growing number of fans. This collection would eventually be published as *Chronicles of Avonlea*. Each of the stories chosen represents a significant mass of similar tales that did not go into the collection. Together the stories chronicle Montgomery's moods, reflect her reading, and illuminate her life in Cavendish over these few lonely years.

Reading the stories in *Chronicles of Avonlea* in their original order of publication in small magazines provides a chronology of Montgomery's developing style and themes. The titles of these magazines reflect another pressure — her need to write for a known market. From "Little Joscelyn," first published in September 1904 in the Boston *Christian Endeavor World*, to "Each in His Own Tongue," printed in *Delineator* in October 1910, the stories reveal Montgomery's growing technical expertise. One British critic, according to Montgomery's 1 March 1930 journal, praised "Each in His Own Tongue" as one of the finest stories in the English language.

As she revised the stories to tuck in references to Anne, Montgomery was living through the last phase of her seclusion on the Macneill farm. In March 1911, changes occurred rapidly. At the age of eighty-seven, Montgomery's grandmother, Lucy Woolner Macneill, died suddenly of pneumonia, following a bout of grippe.

The death of her grandmother freed Montgomery to marry Ewan Macdonald. Within a week, Montgomery and her aunts had dismantled the old house, giving away bits of furniture and burning the personal accumulation of over sixty years. Montgomery moved out, first to the Cavendish manse, then to Park Corner, the home of her beloved Aunt Annie and Uncle John Campbell. Her cousin Stella was there, as was George, his wife Ella, and their little boy Dan. Clara had moved to the United States and married. Frederica — "Frede" — the youngest of the Campbell cousins, with whom Montgomery had recently forged very strong ties of affection and sympathy, came up from Macdonald College near Montreal for the wedding. It was held without fanfare on 5 July 1911, in the living room of the Campbell home. The Reverend John Stirling of Cavendish officiated, and a small group of neighbours and relatives attended. Immediately afterward, the Reverend Ewan Macdonald and his new bride left for a honeymoon in Scotland.

Writing months later about her emotions on her wedding day, Montgomery remembered strange feelings of rebellion and despair. "Something in me — something wild and free and untamed — something that Ewan had not tamed — could never tame — something that did not acknowledge him as master — rose up in one frantic protest against the fetters which bound me" (*Selected Journals* 2: 68).

LEASKDALE

Hunger for a home and hearth had been a central theme of *Anne of Green Gables, Anne of Avonlea,* and a great many of Montgomery's short stories. Among the moving moments in her account of her two-month honeymoon in England and Scotland is the story of her finding two china dogs, reminiscent of those that sat on her grandfather Montgomery's mantelpiece: she imagined placing them in the Leaskdale manse to preside over her hearth. And on the banks of the Tweed, in Walter Scott country, she dreamed of "arranging furniture in Leaskdale Manse" (*Selected Journals* 2: 73).

Homeward bound, the newly married couple travelled via New York and Toronto, where they visited Montgomery's long-time literary acquaintance Marjorie MacMurchy, and Uxbridge, where Ewan's friends from his maritime days, the Reverend Edwin Smith of Whitby and the Reverend J.R. Fraser of Uxbridge, welcomed them. They then took the seven-mile road to little Leaskdale.

If the congregation did not know in advance that their minister's bride was a best-selling author, awareness had certainly dawned by the time of her arrival. The Uxbridge *Times* reported: " 'Despite torrential rain, the Leaskdale church was filled to capacity on Tuesday night [3 October 1911] to welcome the Rev. Ewan Macdonald and his bride, the well-known writer, Miss Montgomery of Prince Edward Island' " (qtd. in Mustard 3).

The manse was nicely situated near a pretty side road. It had a good study for the minister; the minister's wife, however, would have to do her novel writing at the dining-room table. The house had no indoor bathroom or toilet, but it had a neat kitchen

The newly married couple: the Reverend Ewan
Macdonald and L.M. Montgomery in 1911.

Leaskdale Manse, circa 1911.

and a large pantry. When the elegant new furniture arrived from Toronto, the "longed-for home [became] an accomplished fact" about which the new bride could say, "I am — for the most part — content" (*Selected Journals* 2: 87).

The proximity of Toronto would prove valuable over the years, particularly when Montgomery became free to meet publishers and fellow authors there. Immediately, however, there was little time for city outings. The many church families had to be visited and in turn entertained at the manse. Sunday school classes and the young people's guild had to be taught, and three local mission societies and regular midweek prayer meetings had to be attended. Vastly more important, within two months of settling in at Leaskdale the bride found that she was pregnant.

Nevertheless, she worked her way through the last stages of readying *Chronicles of Avonlea* for publication, and as spring approached began work on *The Golden Road*, a sequel to *The Story Girl*. The printed copy of *Chronicles of Avonlea* arrived on 30 June 1912; Chester Cameron Macdonald was born on 7 July. Although naturally somewhat fearful of the whole process, the thirty-seven-year-old mother had an easy delivery and a consequent period of intense elation. Her happiness was increased by the presence of cousin Frede, an increasingly dear confidante.

THE GOLDEN ROAD

The Golden Road was finished in May 1913 and published in September. The first copies arrived while Frede was again visiting on her way to a new teaching position at Macdonald College near Montreal. To young readers, *The Golden Road* appears one of the funniest of Montgomery's books. The jokes, anecdotes, and doings of the group of *Story Girl* children who reappear in this book all appeal to preteen readers. Today's children are less likely to respond to the sentimental sections — the sappy romance of the Awkward Man and sweet Alice Reade — or to the blatant pathos of the treatment of Cecily, whose pretty feet will never leave the golden road of childhood. But again Montgomery had swept a wealth of story into the framing narrative of happy days in an extended family of loving, competing, and changeable kids. Certainly in its own day the book was almost as great a success as its predecessors.

Montgomery wrote this book under the pressure and novelty of a new baby in her life. Given her recent marriage, the two adult romances in *The Golden Road* are intriguing. Aunt Olivia, long thought of as an old maid, attracts a suitor — rather an inglorious one, but one the children can respect. More important is the story of the Awkward Man and Miss Alice. As the music teacher who comes to the King farm to teach the girls, Alice Reade springs from Montgomery's memories of her own role and status during the time she lived with the Campbells. The Awkward Man wins Alice by revealing the secret in his locked room: in his home he has created a shrine for his love. Like the secret room, the wedding scene, with the children strewing flowers, forms for Montgomery a dream alternative to the actualities of her own courtship and marriage.

On the appearance of *The Golden Road*, Montgomery was invited to address an audience of eight hundred at the Women's Canadian Club in Toronto, the first of many such public appearances, events she experienced as both nerve-wracking and exhilarating. She had now begun work on a third "Anne" book. Progress, however, was halted by the onset of a second pregnancy. This time she was miserably ill throughout the nine months, and the outcome, on 13 August 1914, was a stillborn child, a boy given her loved father's name of Hugh and buried with terrible grief.

ANNE OF THE ISLAND AND THE END OF A CONTRACT

Adding to her personal sorrow was the horror of hearing, on 4 August 1914, that England had declared war on Germany. This of course involved imperial Canada. Volunteers hurried to enlist

Frederica Campbell, Montgomery's beloved cousin Frede.

for service overseas, among them Montgomery's half-brother, Carl Montgomery, from Prince Albert. In the face of all this stress, Montgomery finished a story tentatively titled "Anne of Redmond" — published months later as *Anne of the Island* — in November 1914, just before her fortieth birthday.

Superficially, *Anne of the Island* is a college story, an account of Anne's four happy years at "Redmond," the fictional name for Dalhousie University in Halifax. There were few such "college girl stories" at this time; Jean Webster's *Daddy-Long-Legs*, published some years earlier, is one of a very few. *Anne of the Island* contains interesting material on the life of young women undergraduates in the very first years of women's admission to institutions of higher education. Professors, examinations, deadlines, and essays all appear fitfully, but the main interest is the way the college girls live together, setting up house in a cosy little cottage near the park, entertaining friends, male and female, finding nice young men to flirt with and become engaged to.

Like Montgomery, Anne faces the difficult task of choosing between two suitors. Gilbert Blythe's personality in some ways reflects that of the young Will Pritchard, that blithe comrade of Montgomery's Prince Albert schooldays. Royal Gardner seems at first to come straight out of schoolgirl dreams of a handsome, well-spoken, courteous — and rich — Prince Charming, but something chilling in his perfection eventually turns Anne against him. Perhaps there is a trace here of the way Ed Simpson, with all his obvious suitability, failed to warm Montgomery's feelings.

While these and other romances progress, Anne and her friends make a home for themselves at "Patty's Place," where two china dogs sit on either side of the hearth. This is a happy, breezy book, reflecting the author's sense of having found a home, reflecting also what was the major new emotion in her life, her deep love for her chum and confidante, Frede Campbell. Just as friendship furnishes the principal emotion in *Anne of the Island*, Frede was now filling Montgomery's need for companionship, sympathy, and devotion in real life.

Montgomery's eldest son, Chester, as a toddler.

Frede had spent Christmas 1914 at the Macdonald manse. Then, back in Montreal in April 1915, she contracted typhoid. An anguished Montgomery hurried to Montreal to help Frede pull through the nearly fatal illness. In July the cousins shared a holiday at Park Corner, walking and talking near the seashore. Montgomery returned to find the first copies of *Anne of the Island* waiting for her. With the publication of this book, her five-year contract with L.C. Page of Boston was ended.

DOMESTIC DISTRACTIONS

The yearning for another child to assuage grief over Hugh's death was eased in October. Ewan Stuart was born easily and in good health on 7 October 1915. Although Stuart and Chester, the latter now a toddler, kept their mother busy and happy, and church work occupied her afternoons and evenings, Montgomery settled into a professional work schedule, writing every morning. The small boys were trained not to interrupt. There are moving stories about little hands pushing flowers under the closed dining-room door to get the attention of their busy mother, thoroughly engrossed in her imagined world.

In retrospect, this period would seem to Montgomery to have satisfied her longings for an "Ingleside," a home of her own. She had a comfortable house, a pretty garden, a neighbourhood in which she had status, and a writing space where she could do her literary "spade work," block out her chapters, and enjoy the happy spinning-out of her fiction.

There was a disheartening side to domestic life, however. Ewan Macdonald, who to his congregation appeared amiable and competent, was proving to be a disappointing mate. Perhaps Montgomery had hoped for someone more like her enterprising father, a man who could match her own energy. She recorded in her diary that hers and Ewan's intellectual incompatibility precluded a satisfying relationship.

Montgomery began work on *Anne's House of Dreams* in June 1916, incorporating many details from her experiences of the preceding year. In this novel Anne and Gilbert are married. Anne gives birth to and loses a daughter, experiences intense friendships, rejoices at the birth of a son, and accepts the loss of a fatherly mentor. The surface story is essentially a happy one. The subplot, however, concerns another woman, trapped in a meaningless marriage: passionate, colourful Leslie Moore is married to a handsome man who through an accident has become a being without mind or personality.

Anne's House of Dreams is unified by the symbolism of houses: Anne's seashell of a house is set in a garden by the sea, and is the scene of her firstborn's death; Leslie Moore's dark unhappy home is hidden by tangled willows, and in it she is entombed with a brain-damaged husband she loathes; the old storyteller, Captain Jim, lives alone in a lighthouse, with his memories of a bride who never came. An outsider named Owen Ford, a writer coming into Four Winds Harbour, becomes a catalyst in the untangling of tragedies. The book is complex and subtle, a far cry from the little romances of Montgomery's apprentice period.

This novel reveals new ambivalence in Montgomery's vision. The story of Anne Blythe in *Anne's House of Dreams* offers a misted glimpse of the death of a child, marital strains, repression, jealousy, and loneliness. Powerless before the monolithic forces of a religious code of duty and a social code of propriety, Montgomery's characters repress passion, imagination, and personal desires. Yet, this book in the end is full of dreams fulfilled: Anne's second child is born alive; Leslie is released from her marriage tomb; Captain Jim's sad memories are transformed into a book that will live forever. Dreams — composed of memories, desires, and fears — must give way to reality. The characters who suffer most enter new lives, but they give up something of themselves in the process.

Montgomery wrote the novel in a long series of two-hour morning stints, devoting the rest of her days to the boys, to household duties, and to the growing burden of Red Cross war work, mission society meetings, choir rehearsals, and congregational visits. Housekeeping in that era was far from easy.

Woodstoves and coal furnaces challenged a compulsive desire for cleanliness, and there were no washing machines or dryers, no vacuum cleaners or handy dry cleaners or laundries in Leaskdale. Providing ample and tasty food was also a necessity, especially in a minister's hospitable home, but there were no canned goods, no preplucked chickens or processed hams. The corner store in Leaskdale offered flour and sugar and the new-fangled self-rising baking powder — from there on it was up to the housewife to produce cakes and cookies, puddings, pies, and bread, all light and delicious, however heavy and resentful the heart of the hostess.

These were unavoidable and petty irritations. But by the time she finished *Anne's House of Dreams* in October 1916, Montgomery's own house had begun to be invaded by more monstrous disruptions.

LEGAL BATTLES

On 22 February 1916, Montgomery recorded in her journal the first of a series of portentous dreams. The dream involved an alarming storm, a frenzied search for Ewan, and the entry into the house of a running man, a soldier in khaki. The dream stands at the beginning of a four-year period of worry, trouble, and loss. By the end of 1920 the manse at Leaskdale would be battered by a succession of storms.

First, a private war erupted between Montgomery and her American publishers. She had decided to give the Toronto firm of McClelland & Stewart the Canadian rights to her books. After some negotiation, she revised her decision, choosing to contract with them as her primary publishers and dropping the Page connection. Page threatened to sue, claiming he had legal right to a further contract. The threat became a reality, and Montgomery was caught in a legal conflict that would last for over a decade. Meanwhile, McClelland & Stewart published *Anne's House of Dreams* in July 1917. Page retaliated by withholding one thousand dollars in royalties on Montgomery's previous works. Montgomery in turn engaged the attorney of the American Authors' League to defend her cause.

Something of the impetus to change publishers had come from Page's lack of support for Montgomery's desire to publish a book of poems. McClelland's readiness to bring out *The Watchman and Other Poems* in 1916 helped convince her of the sympathetic bond that could be formed with this Canadian publisher. She had worked hard at developing skill in versification during her apprentice period. *The Watchman and Other Poems* gathers and reprints fifty poems published since 1899, together with thirteen new poems. But Montgomery's variety of poetry was going sadly out of style at this period — a time when a new generation of disillusioned poets were turning for themes, vocabulary, and rhythms to the dark urgencies and syncopations of war. Montgomery's pretty, well-turned verses had a wide following, but they were not the sort of thing critics and reviewers were looking for in 1916.

When in 1917 Montgomery published a fragmentary autobiography in *Everywoman's World*, it was partly in defence of her own claim to respect as a writer who had achieved considerable fame — in spite of rather condescending treatment by academic reviewers. She titled her autobiographical sketch "The Alpine Path" and wrote, with justification, of the great self-discipline involved in following a professional writer's path in the face of discouragement and rejection. Writing the article strengthened her sense of purpose and vocation. It also revealed her continuing delight in the wide audience always clamouring for "more L.M. Montgomery."

WARTIME IN LEASKDALE

Rainbow Valley was begun in the fall of 1917 and finished on 24 December 1918. The happy picture of Anne's family life with her six healthy children is balanced here by the story of another family: the abstracted minister in Glen St. Mary who brings up

Montgomery's half-brother, Carl, with her son Stuart in Leaskdale, Ontario.

his children as a single parent. This secondary story hints at the growing abstraction of Ewan, whose increasing withdrawal from family responsibilities had left his wife with the sense that *she* was playing the role of a single parent.

On the edge of the lives of these two families moves a loner, an orphan like Anne, but unlike Anne a pale, hard-edged creature, with an exaggerated sense of her own importance. This orphan, Mary Vance, is the negative, not only of Anne, but also of the Story Girl, that vivid source of value and vitality. Mary Vance is the shadow figure that Montgomery dreaded in herself: sharp, carping, critical. It is as though in creating Mary Vance she was trying to ward off that side of herself, a side that would emerge increasingly, and insidiously, in her diaries.

Montgomery herself moved like a troubled shadow as the news of the war became unremittingly bad. One after another, young members of the Leaskdale congregation went overseas; six of them, including Allan Mustard, Goldwin Lapp, and Morley Shier, were killed in action. The minister and his wife had to console inconsolable families. Montgomery worried herself into a frenzy as the news of battles and retreats surged into the house from the daily papers. Her nervous condition expressed itself in an obsessive watching for battle reports. She pored over maps of Belgium and France and agonized over the forced retreats of the Allied forces before German military might. In June 1917 her half-brother, Carl, had his leg blown off at Vimy Ridge. Crippled, he was sent home, bringing the horrors of war closer.

A wartime wedding — Frede's surprise marriage in 1917 to a young officer in the Princess Patricia's Canadian Light Infantry — was a shock of a different kind. But Frede's husband, Cameron MacFarlane, went overseas at once, and she was free to travel to Prince Edward Island with Montgomery and the boys in the summer of 1918, a holiday visit that would further seal the closeness between them. When the armistice came, it found the cousins together again on the Island, called back by the sudden death of Frede's brother, George Campbell, another of the merry cousins of Park Corner. When George died of the terrible postwar influenza that was sweeping the world, he left a young widow and children, as well as his mother, Aunt Annie, with very little support — and with increasing need for help from cousin Maud.

FURTHER STRESSES

In her professional life, Montgomery moved from that sad scene to a different kind of stress. She was called to Boston to testify in a suit she was bringing against Page for his fraudulent withholding of royalties and his illegal selling of reprint rights without her consent. The trial was gruelling. The Boston court case ended with the judge deciding in her favour on the first count and ordering Page to repay the thousand dollars in royalties he had withheld. As to the resale of reprint rights, here the judgement went against her, since she had already accepted cheques from the reprint house of Page's choice. The major victory was hers, however. To head off any further legal battles, she agreed, out of court, to sell to Page all rights to the books he had published. After some bargaining, she accepted $18,000. It was a good sum at the time, but in the long run Montgomery proved to have made a terrible bargain. Over the years she had to watch Page reap enormous rewards. Not only did the *Anne* series increase in worldwide popularity, but the profits from all movie and stage adaptations went to Page — a great financial loss to Montgomery. (In fact, after paying her $18,000, Page immediately sold the first motion-picture rights for $40,000.)

Near the end of the post-trial dickering, a telegram from Montreal brought Montgomery the dreadful news that her dear cousin Frede had been stricken with influenza. Frede's friends called Montgomery to come at once, hoping she could rally Frede as she had done four years earlier. She rushed to Macdonald College, but this time to no avail: she had the horror of watching the woman she loved so deeply slide into death. Frederica Campbell MacFarlane died on 25 January 1919, victim of the same flu epidemic that had carried off her brother George just a month earlier. Nothing could be more poignant than Montgomery's cry of grief in her 7 February journal: "Oh, my God, can it be true?"

As the sad winter wore on, Montgomery began to copy out her old diaries into volumes of uniform size. In part this was to keep her writing habit going in the pause before beginning another novel. The copying of the diaries also marked her recognition of what a phenomenal resource the old journals were — a unique record of thirty years in the daily life of a woman who combined professional growth with the unfolding events of girlhood, courtship, marriage, motherhood, and housewifery. Perhaps it marked also a subconscious recognition that with the end of World War I a phase of human history was ended; the journal, recopied into permanent form, would stand as a memorial of prewar life.

THE WAR IN WRITING

In March 1919, at a time haunted by bitter loneliness for Frede, dead only two months earlier, Montgomery began *Rilla of Ingleside*. Rilla, Anne's youngest daughter, is presented as the almost unnoticed child in a big family — as Frederica Campbell had been in the early happy days at Park Corner. But this book is no regional idyll. It is, instead, a strong, significant look at the impact of war on the lives of women. Dramatically unready for the interruption of her pretty youthful pleasures, Rilla is tumbled into wartime acceptance of a difficult nurturing role.

Montgomery's journal entries during the war years served as a rich resource for this novel. The war had officially ended four months earlier, but demobilized soldiers were only now arriving in Canada. In the heat of near memory, Montgomery created a unique sense of the sweep and change of events over the past four years. Her book begins on the day that war breaks out, over an obscure act of national terrorism in Sarajevo, and the first chapters suggest the frightening acceleration of the conflict. The British retreat into Belgium in 1914 coincides with the rapid mustering of Canadian recruits: in khaki a week and two days after they volunteer, on their way overseas a fortnight later, without embarkation leave. Subsequent chapters condense overseas events over the next three years, the drag of suspended action alternating with sudden hammering offensives — all set against a sense of the manipulations of politicians in the fighting nations, and an even stronger sense of the lower-key, comic, pathetic life on the home front. No novel in English more effectively groups and organizes wartime events into a comprehensible sequence while combining so movingly the public and private battles.

Rilla, the home-front protagonist, is no Anne: her distinguishing lisp marks her inability to articulate her feelings. Her flowering is darkly delayed, blighted by the loss of one beloved brother and the crippling of another. But like the larks bravely singing in John McCrae's famous war poem, "scarce heard amid the guns below," Rilla's blithe spirit flies toward love at the novel's end. Montgomery's potent mixture of realism (in setting, event, and characterization) and sentimentality produces a book unique among war novels since it presents war as half the world experiences it — from the woman's point of view. It also charts the way in which women contributed to the war effort on the home front, developing capabilities hitherto suppressed.

EWAN'S FIRST COLLAPSE

The composition of *Rilla* was interrupted by Ewan's devastating mental collapse. From complaints of headaches and weakness, Ewan drifted into manifestations of deep clinical depression. He believed himself damned to eternal punishment, not for any particular sin, but within the context of the Calvinistic theological doctrine of predestination, which held that certain unlucky people were predestined to an afterlife in Hell and that good works could not reverse this. The local doctor diagnosed a nervous breakdown and Montgomery arranged a consultation with a Boston nerve specialist. There, in July 1919, Ewan's condition deteriorated and his wife had to make swift arrangements to leave the house, the children, and her own work to go by train to Boston to help him.

Sessions with the doctor, who administered sedatives and other drugs, barely palliated Ewan's condition. Under this new stress, Montgomery learned to depend on sleeping pills in order to get enough sleep to face the troubled days. Since 1904 she had occasionally taken veronal, a barbiturate prescribed for insomnia and mental disturbance, but as she wrote on 27 June 1919, "Realizing fully the danger of forming a drug habit I have never allowed myself to take it, save in cases of great emergency . . ." (*Selected Journals* 2: 331).

The Boston nerve specialist prescribed chloral for Ewan, a drug then used to induce sleep and alleviate the effects of mood swings. In five weeks Ewan was able to return to Leaskdale, his delusions apparently quieted. But for the rest of his life this mental malady would return, each time in more devastating form. Montgomery would henceforth date the end of her happiness at 1919.

In September 1919, after a terrible summer, Ewan recovered from his melancholia as swiftly as he had succumbed. His emergence from the state of delusion, terror, sleeplessness, and pain coincided with a visit from his old Island friend, the Reverend Edwin Smith. Smith had volunteered at the onset of the war and had achieved a fine war record as an officer in the British navy. He had returned to peacetime Canada, but not to the ministry: his present work was in an insurance company in Oshawa, although he remained available as a substitute preacher for ministers unable to preach (as Ewan Macdonald often was and would remain). In this and subsequent visits, Montgomery found herself able to speak freely to Edwin Smith about her many ideas, speculations, and experiences.

Ewan suffered a brief relapse in November 1919, while Montgomery, in the spring of 1920, experienced a revival of her war with the Page company. In spite of the termination of their contract in 1916, Page was determined to publish one more book by Montgomery — a collection of early short stories written before 1912 and submitted at his request years earlier. Montgomery had sent him revisions of these stories; Page claimed to have lost the revisions. Now, when she threatened to sue partly on the grounds that the unrevised work was unworthy and would damage her reputation, Page conveniently "found" the lost revisions and went into production. *Further Chronicles of Avonlea* sported a picture of a redheaded girl on its cover, falsely implying that it was a book about Anne. Montgomery got an injunction, but the book appeared anyway.

Montgomery prepared for battle: "[M]y chance of winning is not good," she wrote in her journal on 9 April 1920.

> But there is *something* in me that *will not* remain inactive under injustice and trickery. . . . Besides, the Page Co. need a lesson. They have traded for years on the average woman's fear of litigation and the fact that very few authors can afford to go to law with them. . . . They have done the most outrageous things to poor authors who can't afford to seek redress. (2: 375)

The Boston court battle was sharp and ugly. Montgomery took veronal every night for a drug-induced sleep (she had been carefully limiting her own use of drugs as well as Ewan's for over a year). The arguments centred in part on what constituted red hair, with learned counsel wrestling over prints of Titian's paintings, trying to decide whether the offending cover picture really constituted a pirating of Anne. As the case ended, Montgomery learned that she in turn was to be sued by Page for malicious litigation. Returning home on 8 July, Montgomery found Ewan miserable again.

Then the nightmares seemed to end. On 24 July Montgomery wrote in her journal:

> Thursday night just when Ewan and I were both feeling very rotten, Captain Smith motored in and in no time had us both cheered up. There seems to be something infectiously healthful about his personality — you simply *catch* optimism from him. He stayed all night and we had a very pleasant evening. He and his family are living at Whitby now, so we can be neighborly, as it is only 30 miles away. . . . (2: 386–87).

By 24 August she was gloating: "To-day I wrote the last chapter of 'Rilla of Ingleside'. . . . It is the last of the *Anne* series. I am done with *Anne* forever — I swear it as a dark and deadly vow. I want to create a new heroine now — she is already in embryo in my mind. . . . Her name is *Emily*" (2: 390).

EMILY OF NEW MOON

The essential difference between Montgomery's Emily and her Anne is that Emily is not just incidentally or peripherally a writer. Emily knows from a very early age that the "flash" she experiences, the exultation and flush of creativity, is central to her being. In this new series Montgomery draws, not on her memory of childhood in general, but on her own unusual growth, the intimations of literary power that had filled and sustained her all her life. Her readiness to communicate this experience through the medium of her new protagonist reflects the fact that since the war Montgomery had been steadily recopying the early parts of her diaries. In the process she had become newly aware of how she had maintained her own commitment to writing despite incredible discouragements during her apprentice years in Prince Edward Island. Writing that first "Emily" book in 1921, Montgomery recounted the ways in which her own early and persistent desire to become an author had been sneered at by those who mattered to her.

The battle with Page, meanwhile, raged on, but Montgomery affirmed her own absolute sense of immunity to such opposition when she traced the early intimations of a literary calling felt by her new protagonist. Friendship with the amiable and cheerful Edwin Smith may also have helped maintain the artist in Montgomery, for he admired her sharp mind and conversational ability; in the novel, both Cousin Jimmy and Teddy help sustain Emily after she loses her father's encouragement and companionship. Emily's subsequent discovery that her first lover, Dean Priest, has no interest in her creative work parallels Montgomery's complaints of Ewan's hostility to her writing.

Montgomery felt increasingly lonely in her private world: Frede was dead, and emotional intimacy was not possible with a husband who lapsed into frequent mental illness and who had no intellectual interests outside of theology. Nevertheless, custom required that she always put on a smiling face for public view. When in August 1921 one parishioner commented that she always seemed so bright and happy, she reacted — though only in the privacy of her journal — "Happy! With my heart wrung as it is! With a constant ache of loneliness in my being. With no one to help me guide and train and control my sons! With my husband at that very moment lying on his bed, gazing at the ceiling and worrying over having committed the unpardonable sin!" (3: 16).

Two days later she wrote the first chapter of *Emily of New Moon*. It took six months to complete — the shortest time of any of her novels. A Leaskdale man, who was a boy in those days, remembers Montgomery at that time, laughing and talking to herself as she worked out her dialogues, while little Stuart and his friend slid down the hall banister a few feet away.

The *Emily* series probes deep into a child's conflict with an authoritarian social structure that fails to fulfil her psychological needs. Emily is a female artist enduring the negative pressures arising in the late nineteenth century, pressures based on the notion that art was frivolous and that a young woman ought at any rate to marry and subordinate her ambitions to those of her

Montgomery in Leaskdale, circa 1922.

husband. Emily initially resists these pressures. She writes, regardless of the hostility of aunts and neighbours; she also exercises strange psychic powers. Montgomery thus uses her new protagonist to personify not only her own creative urge, but also the flash of intuition linked with that creative power.

Another young girl is featured in this novel: Ilse, an anarchic double who acts out her dreams of freedom from restraint instead of sublimating them, as Emily and her creator did, in creative writing.

A LOCAL LAWSUIT

Emily of New Moon was finished on 15 February 1922. Two weeks later another irritation loomed. The previous spring Ewan's car had collided with that of a resident of Zephyr, the site of Ewan's second ministerial charge. The farmer, named Marshall Pickering, was an important man in the local Methodist church. Now, in late February 1922, Pickering decided to sue Ewan for damages to himself and his wife resulting from the accident.

Months of scuttling around gathering evidence and subpoenaing witnesses ensued. Nevertheless, in May Montgomery began "Emily ɪɪ" — the sequel that would become *Emily Climbs*.

That summer, while the idea for this further story about a child with literary talent was still incubating, the Macdonalds had a brief and idyllic holiday in the Muskoka Lake district of Ontario. Montgomery responded intensely to the beauty of the lakes and islands around Bala. In a rare freedom from parish worries, she had the leisure to fantasize about life in this Ontario retreat. The idea for her adult novel *The Blue Castle* had its inception here.

The romantic dream, however, was set aside on the Macdonalds' return to Leaskdale. Battle against the Pickerings raged. Ewan's lawyer offered a small settlement to compensate for damage to the Pickerings' car, but the plaintiff claimed severe damages both to his and his wife's health. The case came to court in November 1922; the Macdonalds were humiliated when the

Toronto judge decided against Ewan and awarded the Pickerings some $3,000 in damages. Ewan, both the driver and the nominal owner of the car, declared himself unable to pay this amount. The judgement was only against Ewan, and he insisted that his wife not pay for him from her (considerable) earnings as an author. In response, Pickering's lawyer tried unsuccessfully to seize the minister's salary. The trial and its aftermath furnished lively material for Montgomery's journal, but it darkened the Macdonalds' subsequent days in Leaskdale.

THE QUESTION OF CHURCH UNION

Indeed, their lives were already dimmed by another problem. In 1923 the General Assembly of the Presbyterian Church voted for union with the Methodist Church. Parliament passed a Church Union Bill in 1924, but the Canadian Senate amended it to allow each Presbyterian congregation to vote on whether to join the new United Church or to continue as Presbyterian. Ewan Macdonald decided to oppose church union and worked strenuously to persuade local people to vote against it.

By March 1924, Ewan, with litigation defeat by the Pickerings still haunting him and religious politics threatening his future, was in the grip of another attack of melancholia. This attack of depression was so intense his wife could barely conceal it from his congregation. Her normal practice was to give out stories about his severe "headaches," to arrange for substitute preachers when he was unable to perform, and to cover for him in innumerable ways during his weeks of debilitating attacks. How could she maintain this façade? She dissembled well, appearing to a reporter for the Hamilton *Spectator* on November 1924 "altogether a delightful person . . . with thick hair slightly graying, which she wore waved and coiled becomingly about her well-shaped head. Her face was unlined and she smiled easily. . . . The large pearls which she wore in her ears accentuated the clear whiteness of her skin" (*Selected Journals* 3: 208).

In spite of her problems, Montgomery's personal fame was climbing. With the appearance of each new book, she gave a series of public talks to the women's clubs in various towns and cities, signing copies of her books — new and old — in bookstores. Continued public acclaim for her work and national recognition by fellow authors helped Montgomery maintain her equilibrium in the face of dreadful private turmoil. When she recorded Ewan's relapse in March 1924, the same journal entry celebrated her completion of the second "Emily" book.

In April she made a brief start at something quite different — the adult romance that would become *The Blue Castle* — but "couldn't get in the proper mood" (*Selected Journals* 3: 180). By May she had returned to her more familiar strain and was gathering material for a third book about Emily.

The summer of 1924 was darkened by the death of her beloved aunt, Annie Macneill Campbell of Park Corner, the mother of Frederica Campbell. Montgomery had been returning to Prince Edward Island virtually every summer, each time enriched by strengthening friendships with May and Alec Macneill (on Pensie's old farm) and Ernest and Myrtle Webb (at the house that had been the model for Green Gables). This time the Island visit was a sad one. And yet a cousin could explain: " 'Oh Maud, you look *so happy*.' " Maud's answer clarifies again the force of that imaginative streak in her make-up — the flash of insight, the gift of articulation that had kept part of her untouched in spite of the tangles in the web of her life: "[U]nder everything in the core of my heart I have always had and been conscious of a certain subtle happiness. . . . With the exception of a few tortured hours now and then it has always been with me . . . that secret realm of imagination and insight" (*Selected Journals* 3: 195–96).

Meanwhile, back home in Leaskdale, the arguments for and against church union continued. Eventually, in January 1925, both of the Reverend Macdonald's churches voted to stay out of the United Church, although the margin in cantankerous Zephyr was very small. The acrimonious aftermath kept ill feelings high in Zephyr, as in many Canadian congregations.

Whenever she could, Montgomery withdrew herself from this conflict. Now that *Emily Climbs* was published, she returned to work on the romance of *The Blue Castle*. She spoke in her journal of her pleasure and joy in writing it: it was a refuge, a daily escape from intolerable realities. It was finished in March 1925, but Montgomery's health was suffering. In the spring of 1925, she recorded in her journal the first of many asthma attacks.

The plot the *The Blue Castle* is triggered by the heroine's ill health. The portrayal of victimized Valancy, put upon and despised by her mother, cousins, and aunts and uncles, terrorized by a doctor's prognosis of imminent death, is handled with dash and grim realism. This oppressed "old maid" of twenty-nine breaks loose from the family, sprung from her servitude by a well-managed plot device: the doctor's foreboding prognosis which frees Valancy from the bounds of social propriety. She moves first to the home of social outcasts, a drunken old reprobate named Roaring Abel and his pathetic daughter, an unmarried mother who has added to public disgrace the private sorrow of losing her illegitimate baby. Valancy moves on from this ménage to a dream home on a Muskoka island, having married a man her clan mistrusts. Her resistance to her clan ripens into open and bitter confrontation.

A major feature of this novel is the appearance for the first time of a convincing male character, Barney Snaith, a funny, bright, opinionated, and energetic man who doesn't moon around like Gilbert and the other young suitors in Montgomery's works. Instead, he rattles up in his car, in company with Roaring Abel. Like the Awkward Man of *The Golden Road* Barney has a secret room. But his is neither a pretty shrine to romance nor, conversely, a gothic Bluebeard's chamber. This mysterious room turns out to be a workshop where he writes popular and powerful books. Barney's work brings his readers comfort, beauty, and consolation: he writes nature studies reminiscent of those by the popular American writer John Burroughs, and he exhibits the same gift of nature-painting as Montgomery herself. Montgomery adds to Barney's glories the fact that he is a millionaire's son. Valancy's bid for freedom from oppression ends with her union to success, authorial power, and wealth — a statement of faith and hope supplementing Emily's conviction of the value of her flashes of insight.

Once again, Montgomery stalled on her commitment to produce the final "Emily" book, one that would require the marriage of Emily. She contracted in July to write four stories about a little girl named "Marigold" for *The Delineator*, an American magazine with a circulation of over a million. Finishing these stories in September 1925, she toyed with the idea of developing them into a book about a child much younger than any of the central figures of her earlier novels.

MOVE TO NORVAL

That autumn of 1925 was a time of major change. Chester, now thirteen years old, left home to go to boarding school in Aurora, north of Toronto. In the church, theological fences had to be mended as many Presbyterian ministers shifted to new positions, merged diminished congregations, or accepted the closing of one charge when two churches merged. Ewan talked vaguely of resigning. Consequently, he was more than ready to accept a call to a different presbytery — to the church at Norval, west of Toronto. Montgomery, who had put down deep roots in her beloved Leaskdale home, felt terrible pangs over the move, although she could see the advantage of a better manse and larger church closer to Toronto. The family moved to Norval in February 1926.

Incredibly, the parishioners of Leaskdale did not suspect the nature of their minister's affliction: his deep and recurring mental illness and his conviction that he himself was damned to

Ewan Macdonald with Ernest and Ida
Barraclough in Norval, Ontario.

eternal hell fire. Montgomery constructed a web of deception. She had given out misleading stories about Ewan's headaches, intimating that these symptoms of his malady were in fact the substance of his health problems. She resolutely refused to seek comfort in confiding her troubles to others; even the maids who worked at the manse were unaware of Ewan's true malady. Only in her journal did Montgomery pour out the truth — not only about Ewan, but about the unbearable distress lurking behind the smiling mask of the competent, cooperative, and cheerful minister's wife. Again and again the journal records her dependence on its pages as a place to let off steam and acknowledge deep-seated worry about the future.

The journal went to Norval with Montgomery as her only confidante.

Norval lies in a pretty glen, where the Credit River forms a fork before running down to Lake Ontario. There were congenial people here and in Union, the other church to be filled by the Presbyterian minister. The new radial train-line made a trip to Toronto a matter of a comfortable half-hour. Life seemed mellower at last, and Ewan's depression subsided for the time being under new stimulation. But Chester began furnishing anxiety: "[T]here are some things about Chester that make me anxious in regard to his future," Montgomery wrote in the summer of that first year in Norval (*Selected Journals* 3: 295). Another worry had also followed them from Leaskdale — worry over the still unsettled judgement against Ewan in the Pickering accident case.

Norval people were proud to welcome a world-famous author as their new minister's wife. She carried with her the half-finished manuscript of *Emily's Quest*, sandwiching work on it between the new duties and experiences of life in an unfamiliar community. Little children who lived on the main street of Norval became used to the sight of the preoccupied Mrs. Macdonald walking down to pick up her mail, mouthing bits of description or dialogue under her breath as she passed, momentarily unaware of village life around her.

At last, by October 1926, *Emily's Quest*, third and last in the *Emily* series, was finished. This book suffers from an interesting tonal disjunction. Montgomery moves from the realist mode of the first two books to a slapstick closure, as if she were undercutting the careful work she had put into building credible situations and believable people. The final section has the theatrical quality of stage farce — perhaps the mark of its author's immersion in amateur theatricals with her church drama group. *Emily's Quest* also contains an essential derailing of its expected ending: Emily's marriage to Teddy is clearly in the offing, but in marrying him she must give up her own calling and prepare to serve as helpmeet, inspiration, and model for *his* art. Perhaps the easier life at Norval had tamed Montgomery's rebellious insistence, through Emily, on the preeminent claims of the writer's art. At any rate, Montgomery's slapstick closure, for many readers, works to undermine its conventional happy ending.

With the move to Norval, Montgomery's own social life was improving. In particular, a close friendship had sprung up between her and one of the prominent parishioners in the Union church. Mrs. Barraclough of Glen Williams, the conventionally devoted wife of the mill manager there, proved most congenial, and her attractive home welcomed Montgomery in a way none of the Leaskdale houses had.

The mail still brought Montgomery daily bundles of fan letters from all over the world. In August 1927, tucked in with those predictable bundles, came a surprising letter from the prime minister of Great Britain, Stanley Baldwin. Baldwin wrote to say that his forthcoming official visit to Canada would be incomplete without a chance to meet the author whose books had long enchanted him. When the prime minister arrived, accompanying the Prince of Wales and Prince George, Montgomery was among the guests presented to the royal party at Toronto. Baldwin drew her aside from the formalities at Government House to tell her how much he and Mrs. Baldwin treasured her early novels.

That fall, while seeing her third "Emily" book through the stages of retyping and proofreading, Montgomery again set to work. The Marigold stories were expanding into *Magic for Marigold*. Working at her Norval bedroom window, the author could look up at a movingly beautiful scene that she called "a hill of pines" (*Selected Journals* 3: 283). This scene merged with the setting she had already imagined for *Marigold* at "Cloud o' Spruce."

The warmer vein of friendship she was experiencing in Norval and Toronto mellowed Montgomery's treatment of women characters. Dr. Marigold Lesley, for instance, brings professional wisdom to the raising of her little namesake — perhaps a reflection of Montgomery's renewed acquaintance with the MacMurchy family in Toronto, in particular, Dr. Helen MacMurchy, director of a branch of the Canadian Department of Health and author of an influential series of "little blue books" about child-raising and nutrition, published by the Dominion government. The emphasis on Marigold's earliest emotions and experiences reflects new 1920s ideas about early childhood education. For the first time, too, Montgomery's child heroine has a loving support-ive mother. Here is the welcoming circle of an extended family, aunts and uncles clamouring to have the little niece for a visit; here too, however, is a child without any trace of the special gifts that characterized Anne and Emily.

In contrast to the happy story about small Marigold was the real story of Chester, beloved first-born, who was now sixteen and causing uneasiness. Chester was girl-crazy, he had taken up smoking, and, as his mother wrote in her journal of July 1928, he was drifting into "something nasty and worrying that embit-tered life for many days and filled us with deep-seated fear of his future" (3: 371–72). Stuart presented a very different worry: the sensitive thirteen-year-old had witnessed a terrible accident in which three beloved village children were killed. On the plus side, summer brought a surprising visit from Ephraim Weber, Montgomery's pen pal of nearly thirty years.

Magic for Marigold was finished in October 1928 and published in 1929. Before 1929 ended Montgomery was enduring physical discomforts — earaches, toothaches, flu, asthma. She had her crowded and painfully abscessed teeth pulled, and at last could smile a pretty smile. She also suffered financial reverses. One company in which she had invested heavily was affected by the October stock panic of 1929. This was the first of a series of reverses which cut deeply into her reserves and made it necessary for her to continue writing popular books. The Macdonalds had never lived on her royalties; the ministerial manse was theirs rent-free, and Ewan's salary paid for food and other basics. The royalty money, however, had always paid for household help, and it had added niceties in clothing, furnishing, and transportation. Now, with first Chester and then Stuart away at an expensive boarding school, family financing came to rest increasingly on the sale of her books. Of course the local parishioners knew nothing of these worries.

Three years into their stay in Norval, a series of fires seemed to presage more troubled times to come. When the great flour mill burned down, Montgomery mourned the weather vanes — they had always seemed like friendly fairy-tale gnomes — and the mill light, which had beamed the first impression of warmth when the Macdonalds had come to their new home in company with Mr. Barraclough, the elder designated to meet and welcome them. June and August brought two more fires: the church shed, and then a field, a grass fire set by mischievous children.

Although the Macdonald boys were away at school, Chester was still exhibiting signs of misbehaviour. Other young relatives were also showing a breakdown in values. When the son of Mary Campbell Beaton, Montgomery's old schoolmate, was convicted of fraud, forgery, and theft, Montgomery accompanied her friend on visits to the court and jail.

All these things were recorded in her journal. But when, in 1930, Montgomery decided that she should prepare a typed

The Norval Presbyterian manse.

version of the journals so that both sons could eventually have a copy, she edited out the many references to her breakdowns and worries.

ROMANCE AND REALITY

In October 1930, forty years after her girlhood trip out West to stay with her father and stepmother, Montgomery returned to the Canadian West on a speaking tour. More important to her than the crowds, the speeches, and the signings was her reunion with her friend of those adolescent days, sister of the young redheaded boy whose friendly admiration had remained warm in her memory. Laura Pritchard Agnew came to meet Montgomery at the Prince Albert station, initiating a rapturous reawakening of their old bond. A second meeting with Ephraim Weber added to these stirrings of earlier memories and perhaps awakened her old ambition to write adult fiction.

Montgomery began working on such a novel, *A Tangled Web*. Here a cantankerous, wilful, and manipulative old woman creates tangles in the web of family life by making a great secret of her intentions regarding a family heirloom. The novel satirizes greed, rivalry, self-aggrandizement, and spite — all frailties or vices with which Montgomery was familiar and which she had observed in village life. But Montgomery had learned to diffuse the tension of her internalized anger through laughter. Speaking through this outrageous character, Montgomery could vicariously make assertions forbidden to her as a dutiful minister's wife.

In a more positive vein, the novel also suggests that the old woman's actions, which stir so many malign emotions, may spur romance as well. Indeed, the tangled plot of this amusing book involves a series of studies of love: between young men and women, between older couples, between an old maid and a little boy, and between two stubborn and crusty old bachelors. This multi-plotted novel juggles dozens of stories and a cast of

Stuart, Ewan, and Chester Macdonald in Norval, 1927.

hundreds, and the denouement surprises. Yet Montgomery had by now written so much about love that her writing, even after a sardonic start, eventually turned around to affirm her readership's sentimental expectations.

She was doing some matchmaking herself these days, promoting a romance between Murray Laird of Norval and Marian Webb, daughter of the Green Gables family, who had come to Ontario on a protracted visit and had fallen in love. In recopying her old journals around this time Montgomery had come to the period of her own obsession with Herman Leard and was undoubtedly moved by the memory of that old passion. Conversely, however — and perversely — she was doggedly working to separate her teenaged sons from the Norval girls who had caught their fancy. Chester was now studying engineering at the University of Toronto and his mother was worried about his interest in Luella Reid. Although Luella was the daughter of one of Norval's old Presbyterian families, the Macdonalds did not want Chester to marry until he could support a wife and family. Stuart, still at boarding school, maintained a friendship with another young woman in the congregation — another connection strongly deprecated by his mother. In spite of a lifetime creating fictions about the desire of young people to fend off interference in their lives, Montgomery was now set on managing the love affairs of her sons. Ironically, her journal reveals no sense of the gap between her stance towards her own children and the portrayal of young folk in her fiction.

The tribulations of motherhood contributed to her recurring malaise. "My head has been bad and queer all day," reads a 14 January 1931 entry in her diary. That year Chester failed his first year at university; next he was fired from his summer job in the Sudbury mines. Two words recur in the journals of 1931 with reference to days, news, and life: "hard" and "bitter." By the end of the year, Montgomery suffered a bout of neurasthenia — as bad as the winter of 1907 down home, when she had suffered what she termed a complete breakdown. Her distress was exacerbated by the excessive, neurotic devotion of a lonely young fan in a nearby village who pelted her with adoring letters, unwelcome visits, and pleading invitations. Nevertheless, Montgomery wrote careful, quiet answers to this admirer's passionate letters — as indeed she personally answered every one of the letters that still arrived in a never-diminishing tide.

Early in 1932 she was also worrying desperately about Park Corner farm, that beloved place of her childhood days. It appeared doomed to go out of the family, for the maturing Campbell sons were showing little interest in taking it over. Montgomery had helped their widowed mother sustain the farm while they were growing up, with the expectation that one of the sons would turn it back into a productive business. By chance, she had recently been given a movie camera as a reward for judging a photography contest. Her vivid imagination led to a fantasy of making a film of the old days at Park Corner. Happily she recalled the laughter and warmth of that early home, so completely removed from the repressed, gloom-filled manses of her married life.

PAT OF SILVER BUSH

Like the reunion with Laura Pritchard, another reinstatement of an old friendship added to Montgomery's happy nostalgia. Nora Lefurgey Campbell, who had lived at the Macneill house while teaching in Cavendish, had once collaborated with the young Montgomery on a playful diary — together they had made unfunny events amusing through the sheer bubbling of their spirits. Now Nora was back, having moved in proximity of Toronto. Sharing stories about their sons, the middle-aged mothers giggled their way back to a sense of youthful fun. Out of this slight upturn of mood came the beginnings of *Pat of Silver Bush*.

A creative miracle occurred: Montgomery transcended her troubled present to call forth the fun and warmth of her past. Memories of the happy house at Park Corner, featured in *The*

Ewan and Maud in a happier vein.

Story Girl and *The Golden Road,* resurfaced through the shared gossip with Nora. The centre of the book is the house itself; the major drive for the protagonist, Pat Gardiner, is the urge to save the house, to keep it unchanged. The glorious ending comes in the final chapter when Pat becomes the chatelaine of Silver Bush.

Like Montgomery, Pat is madly devoted to cats and kittens. A proliferation of cats in *Pat of Silver Bush* — Gentleman Tom, Bold-and-Bad, and the tumble of other kittens — reflects the way Montgomery found rich consolation for all her woes in the companionship of her grey cat, Good Luck.

The two major human loves of Pat's life are Bets and Jingle (Hilary) Gordon. The description of Bets accords closely with Montgomery's memories of Laura Pritchard. But in describing Bets's death and Pat's reaction, Montgomery at last drew on her own desolation at the death of Frede, now at a fifteen-year distance. Pat faces Montgomery's agonized question: "How was one to begin anew when the heart had gone out of life?" (316). Then, as Montgomery was part way through the writing of the novel, she heard the devastating news of Laura Pritchard's death in September 1932. *Pat of Silver Bush* was finished in December 1932, but Montgomery's revisions no doubt intensified Pat's response to the loss of Bets by adding grief for Laura to the unforgotten agony of Frede's death.

As for Hilary/Jingle, his surname, Gordon, so close to Gardiner, suggests that he is an alter ego for Pat. Oddly, Montgomery here reuses names from *Anne of the Island,* where Philippa Gordon was Anne's dearest kindred spirit and Royal Gardner her most handsome suitor. Jingle Gordon is also a direct imitation of Johnnie Eames, the "hobbledehoy" youth in Anthony Trollope's *Small House at Allington* (33). (Montgomery's journals record her continuing delight in Trollope's cheerful, well-crafted novels.) Pat's obduracy in refusing Jingle echoes that of Lily Dale in Trollope's story. But Pat is not motivated by unfortunate devotion to another, worthless young man; for her, the real rival to Jingle is her house, the home she cannot face abandoning.

In Judy Plum, the devoted servant, Montgomery creates an

antidote to all the irritating and inadequate maids she had over-seen in her own house. But Judy is also a late version of the Story Girl, a person of infinite narrative gifts. Montgomery endows her with a stage Irish accent, reflecting the contemporary fashion intensified by the popularity of J.M. Synge, Sean O'Casey, and the travelling Abbey Theatre. (This reflected also, perhaps, the fact that many Norval settlers were of Irish or Scots-Irish de-scent.)

The book nearly completed, after a three-year hiatus Mont-gomery made a fall visit to Prince Edward Island in 1932. The trip brought relief from the nervous symptoms that had plagued her for the past two years. Afterwards, she returned to an increas-ingly troubled life in Norval, where, within the year, she would finish *Pat of Silver Bush*.

BLACK GABLES

On 29 January 1933, Montgomery recorded an ominous and puzzling dream which she felt foretold disaster. The next entry, of 5 February, is enigmatic: "It has happened. It is too cruel and unexpected to write about. I have spent two days in hell." After Christmas, Chester had been asked to withdraw from his studies in engineering because he had failed to attend classes and had flunked four courses. His parents decided to give him one more chance to find a profession: they chivvied him into studying all winter and summer at home and then writing exams in George-town to get into a lawyer's office, the required prelude to enter-ing law school. But Chester's academic failure did not constitute the cruellest blow. On 2 December 1933, halfway through his first year in law, he came home to announce that he had secretly married Luella Reid and that they were now expecting a baby.

All Montgomery's hopes for her older son seemed perma-nently destroyed. Luella had been a helper in Norval concerts and Sunday schools, and her father was an important elder in their church, but a daughter-in-law — let alone a grandchild —

Luella Reid and Chester Macdonald, circa 1932.

did not fit into Montgomery's immediate plans for her son. Nevertheless, and in spite of anguished outpourings in her journal, she established the young couple in a Toronto apartment, promised to support them, and in turn extracted a promise that there would be no more children until Chester had completed his schooling.

At this point Montgomery abandoned her lifetime habit of writing up entries in her diary. For three years, from 1933 to 1936, she could not even find comfort in confiding in the journal that had been her confidante and safety valve for almost fifty years. It was 16 September 1936 before she found the strength to recopy the jottings that recorded those three terrible years.

The first of the problems that added to her despair over Chester was an accumulation of worries about Stuart, now eighteen years old and a first-year student in medicine. "He is in danger of making a dreadful mistake," she wrote in May 1933 — and added another outpouring of bias against the girl for whom he had formed a youthful passion. As well, Stuart was endangering his academic year by overindulging in sports and playing too many card games in the residence common room. The boy who had never caused a moment's worry was becoming a source of anxiety.

Ironically, at this time of fear and misgiving during which Montgomery often sank into lassitude and depression, she was working with Marian Keith and M.B. McKinley on a book entitled *Courageous Women*. This was a collection of essays about Canadian women, commissioned by McClelland & Stewart who had published all three of these professional women writers. Completing her share of the essays in *Courageous Women*, Montgomery no doubt contrasted the opportunities open to women in 1933 with her own early entrapment in a mystique of courtship and romance. Women now were challenging their traditional limitations: Ellen Fairclough, the first woman member of a nominating convention in 1934, would soon become a cabinet minister; Agnes MacPhail, MP, meeting Montgomery at a picnic, demonstrated that public life was open to creative talents;

Mme. Thérèse Casgrain was getting national attention with her campaign to enfranchise women in Quebec.

The biographies in *Courageous Women* are rather tepid stories of endurance in the past. But the fragmentary autobiography that Montgomery was still writing — and living — was not tepid. When she later copied out her daily journal entries, she retained the agonized outbursts while consciously weaving in passages of self-justification. Life was becoming desperately difficult. Ewan was in the grip of his religious melancholy again. Furthermore, he had begun to run from one doctor to another, adding, according to Montgomery's 11 June 1934 journal, "electric head treatments" and blood-pressure pills to his increasing doses of bromides, veronal and chloral. Her journal entries for September 1934 became an hourly log of Ewan's condition: he "groaned and maundered"; cried; heard voices; was "sullen, unshaved, vindictive"; "cranky and hateful"; complained of "feeling like falling"; had a "crazy conviction that he is 'forbidden to preach.'"

MISTRESS PAT AND MAUD MONTGOMERY

These troubles returned Montgomery to the dreariest time of her youth, the solitary years when she was immured in the old home in Cavendish. She brooded over her anticipation at that time, her long wait for a resolution of her life after returning to the Macneill farm — eleven years of uncertainty about the future, nervous tension over the apparent need to satisfy community expectations and settle down into marriage.

Again, Montgomery began to write. On 15 January 1934, she went to work on a sequel to *Pat of Silver Bush*. Now she turned her remembered sense of dragging time into romantic suspense; the worries about her sons' entanglements she transformed into a laughing plot about a succession of false romances. *Mistress Pat* took shape, its eleven chapters representing the eleven years of

Pat's life between the time she gains control of her own home and the time she recognizes her love for Hilary Gordon.

Composition of the chapters of *Mistress Pat* alternated with new dramas in actual life. Baby Luella, Montgomery's first grandchild, was born on 17 May 1934. Four days later, Montgomery wrote the happy Christmas chapter of *Mistress Pat*. Likewise, as the journal records distress about Stuart's romantic attachment to his young girlfriend, the novel swings into a comic cautionary chapter about what happens to pretty girls. The journal records lingering irritation at Chester's lack of ambition and his mismanaged marriage; the novel offers a fictional snapshot of Chester in the portrait of Pat's brother Sid, who brings home an unacceptable local girl and announces he has secretly married her:

Sid had brought May Binnie in and announced, curtly and defiantly, and yet with such a pitiful, beaten look on his face, that they had been married that day in Charlottetown.

"We thought we'd surprise you," said May, glancing archly about her out of bold, brilliant eyes. . . . Pat's face seemed to wither as she looked at them . . . at May, flushed and triumphant under all her uneasiness, at Sid, sullen and defiant. (240–41)

When Ewan's mental health worsened — until in June 1934 he was admitted for a three-month stay in Homewood Sanatorium in Guelph — Montgomery wrote the section of the novel in which Pat becomes engaged to David Kirk, a man whose suggestive surname (a Northern English and Scottish word for church), like that of Jarback Priest in the "Emily" books, implies a connection with the ministry. Kirk is a sad, lonely man, shell-shocked in the war. He comes to depend on Mistress Pat for his happiness, though in the novel he frees Pat from her promise to marry him.

Near the end of the novel, Pat's Uncle Horace pontificates on what makes a good book:

"I don't care a hoot for a book where they don't get properly married . . . or hanged . . . at the last. . . . And the heroines. . . . I don't like 'em a day over sixteen."

"But things are often unfinished in real life," said Pat. . . .

"All the more reason why they should come right in books," said Uncle Horace testily. "Real life! We get enough real life living. *I* like fairy tales. I like a nice snug tidy ending in a book with all the loose ends tucked in." (164–65)

Montgomery denies her readers a sixteen-year-old heroine. But she does "tuck in" the loose ends in a startling way: Judy Plum, the storyteller, dies, leaving Pat to live alone; Silver Bush, the house that has engrossed Pat and constituted her reason for existence, burns down; and Hilary Gordon, the long-rejected suitor, returns, ready to take Pat away to a new home he has built for her out West — at a continental remove from the beloved Island.

"Freedom is a glad thing," Pat says after breaking her engagement to Kirk. Yet Montgomery denies her freedom in the end: "The old graveyard heard [what Uncle Horace would have considered] the most charming sound in the world . . . the low yielding laugh of a girl held prisoner by her lover" (338). As ever, Montgomery had given her readers the romance they wanted; but as before, she had added a subtext of death and imprisonment.

CONCEALING DESPAIR

On 30 November, her sixtieth birthday, alone except for an irritating, uncooperative maid, Montgomery wrote the final chapter of *Mistress Pat*. Then, in a state of terrible but concealed despair, images of death recurred — death as a friend, not to be feared. As Judy Plum had put it in *Mistress Pat*, "Death seems rale friendly" (316).

To the Reverend Ewan Macdonald, on the other hand, the thought of death was terrifying. The need to conduct funerals

— there were eleven in Norval between May 1934 and April 1935 — sent him into depths of depression. Similarly, given this condition, his role as minister at Marian Webb's wedding — she was married from the manse on 4 October 1934 — was yet another secret source of anxiety.

New troubles had emerged in the Norval church as well. When Ewan returned home from the Guelph sanatorium, his nervous disorders in remission, he experienced a freak accident that brought him near death. A pharmacist's error led to his taking a poison which had been substituted for his prescription pills. Sheer luck and quick thought on his wife's part, plus fortunate speed on the part of the local doctor, saved the minister's life. But when afterwards no one from the congregation called to find out how Ewan was, the Macdonalds were tipped off to the fact that something was wrong in the parish.

Unknown to the Macdonalds, hostility against them had grown, based partly on a misunderstanding. The Toronto-based Presbytery had sent out a letter about arrears in ministers' salaries. It was a form letter, but the men in the Norval Church Session mistakenly assumed that Ewan had complained about their slowness in paying his salary and had taken umbrage. As well, Ewan's frequent illnesses made many elders doubt he was earning his salary. Resentment spread to include the minister's wife. In a village conspiracy that seems to have the qualities of both stage farce and melodrama, she was ousted from her position as leader of the local drama group. This was a blow Montgomery bitterly resented since she had poured a great deal of energy into organizing and directing the theatrical efforts of the young people of Norval, obviously at the expense of her own interests as a writer. But Ewan, not his wife, was the chief butt of community hostility. The Church Session offered him a leave of absence until the new year, but by February the atmosphere was so hostile that Ewan was forced to resign his Norval and Union charges.

Sadly, the move to get rid of Ewan was supported by the relatives of Chester's wife, Luella — a difficult stance for them since it meant putting the welfare of the church before personal feelings. Coincidentally, Montgomery's concern over Chester's future had now revived; the lawyer to whom he was articled had fired him for failing to come into the office regularly.

Since Ewan Macdonald now planned to leave the ministry, the family would move to Toronto. Thoughts of leaving Norval, recorded in Montgomery's 5 November 1934 journal, were tragic: "My hill, my trees, my garden, the beautiful church I've loved and worked for, the pretty roads all round." Having finished typing up her book, Montgomery began to pack, unhappily preparing to leave her Norval home: "I have been a mouse in the claws of destiny," she wrote in her diary on 15 February 1935. "For a few moments now and then she leaves me alone — just long enough for a little hope of escape to rise in my heart."

CHRONICLES OF RIVERSIDE

The search for a new home in Toronto began. At first it seemed that the family would have to live in rented quarters, but on 8 March 1935, a house agent sold the idea that with careful management the Macdonalds could afford to buy their own house. After a lifetime of living in other people's houses — her grandparents' first, and then the church-owned manses at Leaskdale and Norval — Montgomery found the idea exhilarating.

On 9 March Montgomery recorded in her diary that she had started a new "Anne" book. Such a move had long been urged by her publishers and fans, but the impetus toward a fresh start came from the end of the Norval fiasco — and the need for house-buying funds. "It ought to do well commercially after the film," she wrote, for the 1934 RKO version of *Anne of Green Gables* had been enormously popular. Though it had brought her no income since she had sold the movie rights to the Page Company, Montgomery realized the publicity value of the film. On 11 March, accordingly, she put in three hours of work in the morning on the new "Anne" book.

"Journey's End" at 210 Riverside Drive, Toronto.

Within a few days she was peering in through the windows of a dream house — at 210 Riverside Drive. Set right on the Humber River, at the western edge of Toronto, with a pine-graced ravine and a distant view of Lake Ontario, the handsome pseudo-Tudor house appeared as a welcome "journey's end." To buy it Montgomery sold her stocks, noting in her journal that they would now have to depend on her earnings for everything. As she began plans for decorating and furnishing, she also began rereading the first "Anne" books, hoping to get back into the swing of those earlier Island days.

The urgent need for money was heightened by a publishing shock: Hodder and Stoughton of England, who had brought out the English editions of each Montgomery book since *Rilla of Ingleside*, turned down *Mistress Pat*. Although Harrap's, a reprint company that had been associated with Montgomery's work since 1925, picked up the first British rights, the sense of financial insecurity remained. Another dampener of spirits at this time was the news that Germany, under Hitler, was rearming and threatening war.

Happier news came too: Montgomery received word of her election to the Literary and Artistic Institute of France. Her wry reaction was recorded in her journal entry for 21 March 1935: "I wish the honor would cure my sciatica, banish neurasthenia, and take away all the bruises of my soul and spirit!"

The move to Toronto meant that the boys could now live at home. Chester's wife had taken the baby and gone home to her widowed father in Norval, so both sons would be allotted a room in the new house. Stuart, alas, was also having academic troubles. A brilliant student while at boarding school, and still a national gymnastic champion, he had failed his first year in medicine at the University of Toronto. It seemed good that he could move in with his parents, escape the temptations of residence life at Knox College — and save on boarding expenses.

The seesaw of hope and anxiety — from her sons' troubles to financial problems, from world news to continuing worry over Ewan's mental health — left Montgomery in a perilously fragile state of mind. By 29 March 1935, her life seemed punctuated with "awful fits of bottomless despair. They are so dreadful. I cannot describe them. It seems for just a moment that a black empty gulf of terror opened at my feet, and that moment seems like a century. Fortunately it never lasts longer than a moment." She would later call such moments her "waves," and would never be fully free of them again.

Nevertheless, Montgomery began what she called "spade work" on the new "Anne" book. She worked ideas for individual chapters into short stories, which she sold to the Montreal-based *Family Herald*. (She had sold seven stories to them over the previous two years.) The actual writing of the novel began on 12 August 1935. Once again, she was finding it easy to write.

With fanfare, Montgomery went to Ottawa in 1935 to be made a Companion of the Order of the British Empire — one of the special awards made in celebration of King George v's silver jubilee. At the time of the investiture she stayed in Ottawa with John Sutherland — the "dear old" Jack on whom she had had a crush during her year at Prince of Wales College. Such memories, such rewards, infused romance and high spirits into *Anne of Windy Poplars*, the book Montgomery was now working on. She finished it on 25 November 1935 — in record short time.

RETURNING TO ANNE

Of course *Anne of Windy Poplars* had no plot. It had been designed to fit into the gap between two earlier published novels, covering the years between *Anne of the Island* and *Anne's House of Dreams*. In this bridging novel, there could be no change in Anne and Gilbert's relationship, no change in Marilla's life, no rebirth of Anne's writing career. Instead, Montgomery performs what is really her best trick, creating a series of chapters, each a story unto itself. The story sequence, later glorified by such writers as Alice Munro and idealized by feminist critics as appropriate to the mindset and experiences of women, was imposed in this case by the exigencies of the situation.

Each chapter emerges as a self-sufficient unit, funny or senti-mental or pathetic, although characters link one to another, with Anne and the three old women she boards with forming the running connection. The language has Montgomery's old tang — Miss Courtaloe, for example, commenting on the man who didn't like his wife's hat: "He *et* it. . . . Of course it was only a small hat . . ." (55–56). There is also a refreshed sense of natural beauty, renewed perhaps by the Humberside vista:

> [Anne] slipped through the hall to a back door that opened almost on the bay, and flitted down a flight of rocky steps to the shore, past a little grove of pointed firs. . . . How exqui-site the silver patterns of moonlight on the bay! How dream-like that ship which had sailed at the rising of the moon and was now approaching the harbor bar! (126)

There are the folksy anecdotes — "Nathan always believed his wife was trying to poison him but he didn't seem to mind. He said it made life kind of exciting" (56) — and the schoolday misunderstandings and triumphs. Some characters take shape in Montgomery's memories of her own childhood — Pauline, the old maid whose martinet mother keeps her from social life and pretty clothes; Little Elizabeth, whose grandmother drives her into nervous imaginings; the Pringles, who evidence Simpson oddities. Even Montgomery's neurotic adoring fan from the nearby town appears in silly hysterical Hazel. And of course there is the all-pervading warmth of whimsical, sympathetic Anne.

Moving from Montgomery's journal of the period to this novel is like getting a whiff of fresh air, suddenly sharing a fit of giggles, noticing how pretty young people are, believing in love. How did she continue to invoke that other side of life whenever she moved into the world of fiction?

So many romances, such sympathy for girls who have not found "happy endings," such an authorial disposition to deal out romance to all — these seem strange coming when Montgomery felt such bitter disappointment over her sons' romances. Stuart, in particular, remained very fond of his young friend in Norval — a fine young woman. Montgomery spoke of his attachment with terrible distaste, worrying that he, like Chester, would marry before he could support a wife. Yet the girl was the age of those fictional lasses on whom she lavished such sympathy and tenderness.

Anne of Windy Poplars was published in 1936. The family had enjoyed a pleasant Christmas, a remission in the hammer-blows they had recently endured. Ewan appeared melancholy but not out of touch; Stuart and Chester were nervous about their college exams, but there seemed no real trouble in the wind. Montgomery was enjoying visits to the Canadian Authors' Association and the PEN society in Toronto, while enduring a round of public appearances in connection with her new publication. She read new books, reread some old ones, and enjoyed such movies as *The Little Minister*, based on a book by J.M. Barrie she had first read while at Dalhousie University.

JANE OF LANTERN HILL

In April 1936, Montgomery began spade work on another book. Opening in Toronto, *Jane of Lantern Hill* reflects Montgomery's joy in the new house on Riverside Drive: in the novel young Jane glories first in a perfect house on Prince Edward Island and later in a small house in "Lakeside Gardens" in Toronto.

Yet real life in Toronto was bringing trouble with a vengeance. In May a second grandchild, Cameron Stuart Craig, was born. His coming had been kept secret because there had been so much disapproval of the marriage and Chester had promised not to expand his family. Furthermore, Chester's marriage itself appeared desperately shaky. A more cruel blow than the news of the second child impended: Chester had found a new love in Toronto, Ida Birrell, a girl he had met at the west-end church activities Montgomery had encouraged him to attend.

These were days when the world's newspapers simmered with the scandal of King Edward VIII's passion for Mrs. Wallis

The "dear and sweet" babies: Montgomery's grandchildren,
Cameron ("Macie") and Luella Macdonald, circa 1936.

Simpson — married when he first fell in love with her, divorced (for the second time) when he declared his intention to marry her. Disapproval of divorce, always stronger in Canada than in the United States, hardened — at the very moment when Montgomery had to face the probability that her son would himself be involved in a scandalous divorce proceeding. When Edward VIII abdicated in 1936 to marry "his divorcée," the idea of divorce had become generally invested with a sense of disloyalty and irresponsibility.

After four months of spade work, Montgomery began writing *Jane of Lantern Hill* on 21 August 1936. As the months passed and she enjoyed visits from Luella and the "dear and sweet" babies, Montgomery wrestled to save her son's once unwelcome marriage. However, during that summer of 1936, as she was treating her fictional child, Jane, to all sorts of pleasant gifts, Montgomery was enacting a manipulative and judgemental role in her own family, trying to enforce her ideas on both Stuart and Chester. Knowing this, it seems strangely self-deprecating of Montgomery to have portrayed the villain of *Jane of Lantern Hill* as a selfish and cruel old grandmother who attempts to break up her child's marriage, welcomes the possibility of that daughter's divorce, and is bitterly critical of her grandchild.

At the outset of *Jane of Lantern Hill*, this grandchild lives in Toronto. But as in *The Story Girl* and *The Golden Road*, Toronto is a launching place from which the lonely child can move to the always magic island. A happy autumn visit to the real Prince Edward Island, which renewed Montgomery's sense of its beauty, found its way into the novel: Jane comes, like Anne long ago, and like Bev and Felix, to this place of red roads, apple blossoms, eccentric adults, and lovable cats. Like Montgomery on the day she first saw "Journey's End," Jane and her father — whose surname is Stuart — peer through the door window and fall in love with the house, gasping at the view it opens onto (the Gulf in the novel, the ravine and Lake Ontario in Toronto reality).

Montgomery's new protagonist has none of Anne's uncanny imagination, no flash of creative genius like Emily's — the male

L.M. Montgomery in her garden at "Journey's End" in the late 1930s.

"Dad" is the writer in this story. In this and other respects, he is very much like Barney Snaith of *The Blue Castle*, including the fact that he masks his creative career under a pseudonym. It is, however, not the imaginative "Dad" but the straightforward Jane who defeats the two antagonists — a smiling, manipulative aunt and an icy, judgemental grandmother.

Montgomery contrived for *Jane of Lantern Hill* a new kind of ending — not the conventional boy-girl romance, but a restoration of married love between an estranged couple, Jane's parents. For Jane, this resolution brings with it all the things the young Maud Montgomery had once yearned for: girlhood in the company of a dearly loved father, a potential stepmother safely banished, and the living presence of a tender, understanding mother.

September 1936 brought the sudden death of Ernest Barraclough, the kindly Glen Williams friend whose lavish hospitality and ready sympathy had woven warmth into the Macdonalds' lives in Norval. Struggling to finish *Jane of Lantern Hill*, Montgomery wrote in her 29 September 1936 journal, "I am broken and defeated." And as always, January revived the memory of Frede Campbell's death, adding to the poignant grief over the more recent loss of Ernest Barraclough. In January 1937, Montgomery's beloved cat Good Luck, who had brought her daily comfort and pleasure for over thirteen years, also died — a loss she mourned grievously. In January, too, Chester's infidelity became clear.

Throughout this troubled time, Montgomery was finishing *Jane of Lantern Hill* and typing up the manuscript. She was, however, so dispirited that she did not keep up the habit of writing her journal. She continued to jot down brief notes, but it was January 1938 before she could marshal a year's worth of these jottings into a clearly flowing journal narrative. Like the earlier break in 1933–36, this year-long hiatus in the always-comforting task of writing in her journal signals the extent of Montgomery's troubles and the depth of her nervous prostration.

In the grip of obsessive despair, Montgomery still felt the urge — the necessity — to write. "Tried today to pick out an idea for my next book," runs her note dated 16 March 1937. "If I could get an idea I might gather the material for it while waiting for a return of mental calm." Soon the entries run, "Did spade work," "Did a little spade work," until finally on 26 April, "Did three hours of spade work on 'Anne of Ingleside.'"

But work on *Anne of Ingleside* soon stalled. She could plot and draft but not compose. Small wonder! In late June Ewan entered a spell of madness. As Montgomery wrote in her 11 July 1937 journal: he talked to himself, couldn't remember how to dress himself, and sat for days with "hair bristling, blue underlip hanging down, eyes glaring, face livid." Montgomery kept herself busy with housework, and with a new project of typing up a shortened version of the early parts of her journal. Months of sleeplessness and nervous unrest followed. It was more than a year later before she could stop writing grimly in her now-revived journal, "I *will* write," and enter, in italics, on 12 September 1938, *"began to write Anne of Ingleside.* . . . It is a year and nine months since I wrote a single line of creative work." Sadly, by 27 September, the tune had changed: "Tried to write but had to give up and go to bed."

Many of Montgomery's worries centred on the war scare posed in 1938 by Hitler, eased but not ended by the Munich Agreement. The world was inching toward war, and the mother of two young men could not forget the dreadful toll taken by World War I. Chester joined the 48th Highlanders Reserve and, according to Montgomery's 14 October 1938 journal, "looked splendid in his kilts. Alas!" Stuart, as a medical student, would be exempt from military duty for the time being — but anyone who had lived through World War I could hardly hope that any young man would not eventually be drawn into the armed forces.

Ewan, who was barely in touch with reality by November, spent an entire night orating nonsense with fantastic gesticu-

lations. He was consulting doctor after doctor in a hypochondri-
acal search for relief from his symptoms. All this added unbear-
ably to his wife's nervous tension. She herself had broken a bone
in a fall — one of several mishaps occurring as she aged but
refused to slow down in her household work. Nevertheless, on
28 December 1938, she finished *Anne of Ingleside* — "my twenty-
first book." (Montgomery refused to count *Further Chronicles of
Avonlea*, pirated by Page in 1920, among her productions.)

Many of the troubles of these days are reflected in *Anne of
Ingleside*. Yet again, although the disturbing events of Montgomery's life and memories created the stimulus for her fiction,
all were transformed into a mélange of wit, charm, prettiness,
and warmth. Ewan's neglect emerges as Gilbert's forgetfulness:
he has forgotten Anne's anniversary, not because of a fuddled
mind but because he is too absorbed in the problems of his
profession. The marriage that seemed so dead in real life has as
its fictional counterpart a strong, loving relationship faltering
only briefly over a misunderstanding that dissolves with news of
Gilbert's competence as a doctor: Anne, unlike her creator, looks
forward to the enjoyment of "confidence and peace and delightful work . . . laughter and kindness . . . that old *safe* feeling of a
sure love" (318–19).

With her ear for comic nuance, Montgomery picks up a phrase
used sneeringly by jealous Christine — "*What* a family!" (310) —
and reuses it as Anne exults in serene domesticity: her little boys
sturdy and reliable, safely asleep; her little girls not yet "the
mist-veiled forms of beautiful brides" (322); Anne herself looking forward to a happy holiday with Gilbert. Readers who now
know the truth about Montgomery's situation may well echo
the phrase in yet another tone, applying it to real life with sad
incredulity: "What a family!"

LOSS OF WILL

Lucy Maud Montgomery's continuous journal ends on 30 June
1939. After millions of words and thousands of pages, she set

Chester Macdonald in his kilt, circa 1938.

aside the big, lined ledgers into which she had poured so much of her ambition, depression, irritation, and satiric laughter. She would open the journal again only briefly for a few last truncated entries.

Since *Anne of Ingleside*, Montgomery had done very little creative writing. She had been busy corresponding with her agent, her publishers, and a potential buyer of film rights. RKO had made a good offer for the rights to *Anne of Windy Poplars* and *Anne's House of Dreams* — conceived as promising sequels to the very popular film version of *Anne of Green Gables*. This fortunate windfall would enable Montgomery to put up the money to buy Chester into a law partnership. He had finished his law courses in the spring of 1939, but plans for him to move into a law practice seemed endlessly to form, dissolve, and reform. He settled briefly into an office in Aurora, north of Toronto, near the boarding school at which he had made so fine a start in his academic life. Luella and the children were now with him again, but marital disaster still threatened.

As for Stuart, he graduated in medicine in 1939, and there is a proud photograph of Montgomery with her now satisfactory son. Satisfactory professionally, that is; she was still worrying about his Norval romance, and was eagerly encouraging his interest in a clever, well-educated Toronto woman, a few years older than he was, and — most importantly — the daughter of a prominent neighbour on Riverside Drive.

Since February, Ewan had been in another highly disturbed state, pouring patent medicines into his system, consulting a further series of doctors. A bitter tiff between Montgomery and her maid added to her sense of distress and helplessness. On 27 April 1939, she had thought of starting another "Jane" book, but couldn't whip up the interest.

There is no journal record of her last visit to Prince Edward Island in the summer of 1939; war broke out that September. Only in a few fragmentary letters to her long-time correspondents did Montgomery record her horrified response to the nightmare, twenty years after the end of the "war to end all

E. Stuart Macdonald with his proud mother after
graduating in medicine from the University of Toronto.

wars." She reported to George Macmillan, her old friend in Scotland, that Chester had been turned down for active service because of his poor eyesight, and Stuart placed on reserve until the end of his intern year. But the woman who had agonized over the news of the First World War was only slightly reassured by the temporary immunity of her own family.

In another letter to George Macmillan on 14 March 1940, Montgomery speaks of being "lonely this winter. Chester away in a home of his own, — Ewan is spending the winter in Florida" (*My Dear* 200). This letter reflects Montgomery's nervous strain at the time. Later that spring she fell again and injured her arm, an accident that left her helpless for four weeks, hopelessly worried about her ability to write.

What with these personal worries and the news of the fall of France under invading German armies, Montgomery suffered a devastating nervous breakdown in 1940. Stuart, now an intern at St. Michael's hospital in Toronto, could only help his mother by making quick visits to the house each day; Chester continued to add to her misery with his financial and marital irresponsibility.

Montgomery picked up her old 1936 journal in December 1940 to comment briefly in the margins on her intolerable distress at this time and to add a sharp cry of despair, primarily over her finances. No new novel was in hand to furnish needed royalties; she was, however, collecting previously written stories, all slightly linked by the character of Anne. She tentatively called this collection "The Blythes Are Quoted." (In 1974, Stuart, her literary executor, would publish this collection, minus the linkages, as *The Road to Yesterday*.)

A few downcast letters to her oldest friends, Ephraim Weber and George Macmillan, and to still dearer members of her extended family, such as May and Alec Macneill, illuminate Montgomery's sadness from November 1940 to December 1941. "Oh God, such an end to life. Such suffering and wretchedness," runs a one-line entry added on 8 July 1941 to the neglected journal, her personal life-book. Month after month she struggled to write even a minimal number of letters. Her news was all bad:

the law practice she had staked Chester in had ended with financial loss and professional failure; his marriage to Luella had disintegrated, with divorce to follow; Stuart faced the probability of military service as soon as his internship ended; Ewan's state of mind grew worse and worse; and her sense of despair was taking a severe toll on her physical health. She was now writing in her tenth journal, the one destined to finalize her life-story. One demoralized and fragmentary entry, for 23 March 1942, summarizes her feelings: "Everything in the world I lived for has gone — the world has gone mad. . . ." She saw no space for hope, either in her personal life or in the larger sphere of world politics.

Montgomery attempted a last professional correspondence in 1942, writing to Ryerson Press concerning a Canadian edition of her work, but the correspondence ended sourly. In her final letter to George Macmillan, she told him that her life had been much more unhappy than she had ever confided to him in their forty-year correspondence. The evidence of the journals suggests this was true. Yet the evidence of the novels, as well as the testimony of those who knew Montgomery, suggests equally strongly that her life had been much happier than she ever confided to her journal. As long as she could write about Anne or Emily, or Jane or Pat, she could reenter a world of beauty, whimsy, wit, and idealism. Writing had always given her access to spiritual ebullience. Her joy had inhered in the act of writing, composing, and reworking material so that conversations could sparkle, people stride or bounce or fly, and landscapes glow in the surreal light of imagined starlight or sunshine. When unhappy, Montgomery would insert dark shadows into her novels, but most of that unhappiness flowed into her journals, leaving her novels to record the lives of women dreaming of blue castles and imagining warm inglesides, harbouring gables, and lanterns on the hills of their personal islands. True tragedy came into her life when she could no longer write — neither fiction nor fixative journals.

In 1942, Montgomery's physical and mental health continued to decline, despite regular medication from her doctor and frequent visits from friends. Her husband had become too senile to function rationally; she brooded that the war would take her only "good" son, as she called Stuart; she had wasted away to the point that visiting friends barely recognized her. Much of the time she was bedridden, too weak and unsteady to hold a pen: she was unable to write letters or journal entries, let alone fiction. The will to live was apparently gone.

Death came in the spring of 1942, on 24 April, seven months before her sixty-eighth birthday. Montgomery's treatment of death in her many novels had been one of her strongest achievements. Matthew Cuthbert's death in *Anne of Green Gables*, Cecily's in *The Golden Road*, the death of Anne's poet-son, Walter, in *Rilla of Ingleside* — each had misted the eyes of millions of readers. Her own death had no such artful nostalgia or gentle poignance. We might say, as Shakespeare's character says of King Lear: "[H]e hates him / That would upon the rack of this tough world / Stretch him out longer" (5.3.313–14). Maud Montgomery Macdonald had been torn long enough by racking pain — of mind, body, and spirit.

THE POSTHUMOUS LIFE

Five years after Montgomery's death, a monument was erected in the national park in Cavendish, and another in the small cemetery where she was buried. Green Gables had already become a tourist shrine for hundreds of thousands of visitors. The real Montgomery shrine, however, is her writing: the set of novels — lyrical, exciting, humorous, well-crafted — and the journals — rougher, sadder, but also increasingly showing a sharpening of phrase, a heightening of emotional climax, and a darkening of the shadows of self-portraiture. The tortured self-portrait contained in the journals is perhaps Montgomery's greatest literary creation: it, too, was carefully crafted, by the same skilful hand that sketched the portraits in her novels.

Montgomery's novels move easily between dry wit and broad humour, between mawkish sentimentalism and deadly aimed satire. She carries her readers along with her narrative skills.

Underneath the stylistic interplay, however, her books hold strong power, especially for women. Her light-fingered touch keeps readers chuckling even while they are being swayed by the power of her anti-authoritarian subtexts. In the journals she throws uneasy light on darker aspects of life. Again, the narrative shaping, the comic tang, and the sharp sense of character grip mind and heart.

If only in terms of psychology, the novels and journals together form a fascinating study. In some ways they seem to have been written by two different women. Two recent critical books emphasize the way the novels and journals serve as strangely contrasting mirrors of Montgomery's life. Yet Elizabeth Epperly in *The Fragrance of Sweet-Grass* and Gabriella Åhmansson in *A Life and Its Mirrors* also show that the novels alone contain submerged hints of both sides of the psyche: the whimsical, gentle, happy aspects and a gifted woman's secret resentment at having been pushed into a subservient life wasteful of her talents. The journals, too, show two sides: the woman bending under her cares, and the free spirit soaring in private exhilaration.

People who met Montgomery could easily see her as the author of books celebrating a beautiful world, as a person involved in a circle of loving and lovable people. Indeed, the face she presents in the journals is barely recognizable to people who knew her in real life, or to those who formed an image of her as the author of those beloved fictions. Outwardly warm, generous, upbeat, chatty, concerned with fashion and gossip, Montgomery was inwardly (to judge by the journals) tormented by pain, fury at her husband's ineptitude, and anguish at her older son's increasing strayings. Many who knew her — including relatives who knew her well — have been astonished by the journals: these private writings simply did not reflect the woman they knew. Even her son Stuart, who had been extremely close to her in her final years, was surprised, after her death, by the mother he encountered in the journals.

But if we turn that astonishment around, we return to the novels with a dawning recognition that here Montgomery released another side, equally real, equally surprising, especially given the darkness in her life. The "Anne," "Emily," "Pat," and "Jane" books bubble from an unending sense of fun. They hold their power precisely because they were produced in the knowledge that the world was not a magic island, full of kindred spirits, where love would lead to happiness.

The portraits Montgomery developed in her books probably perverted and distorted her responses to reality. When she turned from the funny eccentrics of her imagined world to the petty corruptions and small-minded malice of Cavendish, Norval, Leaskdale, and Toronto, reality must have appeared most frustrating. She must have wished that life would conform to her imagination — even though she sometimes scoffed at the pink sugar fantasies she spun to please her publishers and fans. The tangy undertones of her novels could not armour her against the sourness of a life she tried so hard to control and dignify.

In fact, both kinds of writing served their author as a "road to yesterday." She used her journal as a path to her own past, a past increasingly darkened by her selective recollections of deprivations, loneliness, enmity, defeat, bad luck, and disappointment. Her novels, on the other hand, provided her with a road to an equally real "yesterday," of brightness, fun, sweetness, and loyalty. The fascinating fact is that both paths begin with the same reality, the same experiences of life — a life not fully captured in either mode, but emerging for observers who study the two together.

We can drop the role of psychologist when we approach Montgomery's literary monuments. We too become imaginative travellers, traversing the dark path or the sunny one, with gratitude for the power of words to lift us into another life, different from, yet shockingly or thrillingly like, our own.

Reading the journals, not as *the* truth, but as *a* truth, a very powerful, persuasive, apparent truth, we can finger their textures, see how the weaver has doubled back on her own design, accepting some of life's tangles and cutting through others. Reading Montgomery's novels, we see her turning the fabric of her life inside out. In *Hamlet*, Ophelia's distraught brother says of her: "Thought and afflictions, passion, Hell itself, / She turns to favour and to prettiness" (4.5.188–89). Montgomery had Ophelia's gift: she could transform the stresses of her life into acceptable, beautiful fictions. Unlike Ophelia, the conversion to "favour and to prettiness" was deliberate — and consummately artful.

Montgomery exits from her journals suffering and silenced, perhaps believing they contained the true and only story of her life. But she was far from defeated — and far from silenced. Witness the millions who still reach for her writing today.

CHRONOLOGY

1874   Lucy Maud Montgomery is born on 30 November into a Canadian family with Scots-Irish-English heritage on the north shore of Prince Edward Island. Her 21-year-old mother is Clara Macneill Montgomery of Cavendish; her father, 33-year-old Hugh John Montgomery of Park Corner, is a storekeeper in Clifton, PEI.

1876   Montgomery's mother dies of consumption. Her father leaves her in the care of her maternal grandparents, Alexander and Lucy Woolner Macneill. She is raised with access to an extended family of aunts, uncles, and cousins.

1880   Young Maud learns to read in the one-room schoolhouse across the Cavendish road from the Macneill farmhouse. She listens to family storytellers.

1883   She begins writing poetry and keeping a diary.

1887   Her father remarries and settles permanently in Saskatchewan with his new wife, starting a new family. A literary society is formed in Cavendish, featuring visiting and local speakers and housing a lending library.

1890   Montgomery travels by rail with her grandfather, Senator Donald Montgomery, to join her beloved father and uncongenial stepmother in Prince Albert, Saskatchewan. She forms strong friendships with Laura and Will Pritchard during her year in Prince Albert and achieves her first publications, in the Charlottetown *Patriot*, the Montreal *Witness*, and the Prince Albert *Times*.

1891–92 Back on Prince Edward Island, she spends part of a year with her Campbell cousins in Park Corner, then finishes school at Cavendish.

1892–93   Montgomery takes a teachers' training course at Prince of Wales College, Charlottetown.

1894–95   Her first year of teaching at Bideford, P.E.I.; includes early morning stints of writing stories and poems. She publishes in Sunday school papers and in the Toronto *Ladies' Journal*.

1895–96   She saves enough money, with family help, to enrol at Dalhousie University, Halifax, for one year. Her first earnings, from Philadelphia's *Golden Days* and Boston's *Youth's Companion*, confirm her belief in her calling as a writer.

1896–97   Montgomery teaches school in Belmont, P.E.I. She becomes secretly engaged to Edwin Simpson, a young Baptist theological student. She begins to sign her short stories "L.M. Montgomery."

1897–98   Teaching at Lower Bedeque, P.E.I., she falls in love with a young farmer, Herman Leard, but painfully rejects the idea of marriage to him. She also breaks her engagement to Edwin Simpson. She continues with her ambitious writing career and publishes 19 stories and 14 poems in the space of twelve months.

1898   Her grandfather's death recalls her to Cavendish to help her aging grandmother. There she learns of two more deaths, Herman Leard's in 1899 and her father's in 1900.

1900–03   Except for a six-month stint in Halifax as copy editor on the *Daily Echo*, she spends the next three years reading, gardening, housekeeping, developing a friendship with Nora Lefurgey, corresponding with pen friends — including Ephraim Weber of Alberta and George Macmillan of Scotland — and writing. Some stories from this period will be reused later in *Chronicles of Avonlea*, *The Story Girl*, and *Further Chronicles of Avonlea*.

1903–05   Friendship with her cousin Frede Campbell strengthens. Her social life picks up after a new Presbyterian minister, the Reverend Ewan Macdonald, is inducted into the Cavendish church. She settles into writing her first novel, *Anne of Green Gables*.

1906   Montgomery becomes engaged to Ewan, although without hope of marriage while her grandmother remains dependent. Her fiancé goes to Glasgow for advanced study, while she turns to work on a serial, later published in 1910 as *Kilmeny of the Orchard*.

1907   L.C. Page of Boston contracts to publish *Anne of Green Gables*; he urges her to begin a sequel.

1908   *Anne of Green Gables* goes through six editions and sells 19,000 copies in its first five months, eliciting fine reviews and letters from Mark Twain, Bliss Carman, and hundreds of other fans.

1909   First of a sweep, *Anne of Green Gables* is translated into Swedish — then into Dutch in 1910; Polish, 1912; Norwegian, 1918; Finnish, 1920; French, 1925; Icelandic, 1933; with six other languages adding translations after the author's death. *Anne of Avonlea* and some 50 short stories and poems are also published this year.

1910   The Reverend Ewan Macdonald moves to Ontario, accepting a ministry in Leaskdale and Zephyr. In Charlottetown, Montgomery is presented to the Governor General of Canada, Earl Grey. She visits her publisher, L.C. Page, in Boston.

1911   Her grandmother dies, aged 87, in March. *The Story Girl* is published in May. Montgomery marries Ewan Macdonald in July and the newlyweds set off on a two-month honeymoon to Scotland and England. They return to set up house in the manse at Leaskdale, Ontario, some 60 miles northeast of Toronto.

1912   *Chronicles of Avonlea*, a collection of early stories revised to include references to Anne, appears in 1912, just before the birth of Montgomery's first son, Chester Cameron.

1913   Montgomery finishes *The Golden Road*, the first of her novels composed in Ontario. She returns for a summer visit to Cavendish and Park Corner and in September begins work on a third "Anne" book.

1914   After a miserable pregnancy, she gives birth to a second son, Hugh Alexander, who dies at birth on 13 August. The beginning of World War 1 adds to her personal sadness, but Montgomery's fiction turns to happy days of college and romance; she finishes *Anne of the Island* just before her fortieth birthday.

1915   Montgomery suffers agonies of fear when Frede Campbell nearly dies of typhoid. *Anne of the Island* is published in July. October brings the birth of a healthy son, Ewan Stuart.

1916   *The Watchman and Other Poems* garners favourable reviews but few sales. Montgomery changes publishers, leaving Page, with whom she is increasingly irritated, and choosing Toronto's McClelland & Stewart for her next novel.

1917   *Anne's House of Dreams* is published. Montgomery also publishes an autobiographical essay, *The Alpine Path*, revealing some of the experiences from which her fiction has been drawn.

1918   Legal battles with Page intensify, first over his withholding of royalties, then over his proposal to publish, without her authorization, a collection of her early stories.

1919   She is devastated by the sudden death of her cousin Frede in January. In May her husband has a nervous breakdown. During the summer, he is treated in Boston by a nerve specialist; in September he snaps back, thanks partly to visits from his old friend Edwin Smith. *Rainbow Valley*, in which Anne's children befriend the motherless children of a minister, is published. *Anne of Green Gables* is made into a film, for which Page legally collects $40,000 for moving-picture rights.

1920   *Further Chronicles of Avonlea* appears with unauthorized revisions of her stories. Montgomery sues Page; the publisher brings a countersuit for malicious litigation.

1921   *Rilla of Ingleside* is published.

1922   A car accident involves Ewan in an acrimonious local lawsuit, launched by Marshal Pickering of Zephyr. The family enjoys a brief holiday in the Muskoka Lake district of Ontario. Judgement goes against Ewan in the Pickering case.

1923   Montgomery wins her case against Page in American courts. Page launches an appeal. *Emily of New Moon* is published. Montgomery is made a Fellow of the British Royal Society of Arts.

1924   The Macdonalds work to persuade Leaskdale and Zephyr people to vote against the union of the Presbyterian and Methodist churches.

1925   *Emily Climbs* is published. Montgomery's eldest son, Chester, goes away to boarding school in Aurora.

1926   The *Emily* series is interrupted by the publication of *The Blue Castle*, an adult romance set in Ontario's Muskoka region. Ewan accepts a new charge in Norval, Ontario.

1927   *Emily's Quest* is published. Ewan's mental health remains unstable. Montgomery is presented to the Prince of Wales, Prince George, and the British prime minister in Toronto.

1928   Her younger son, Stuart, leaves for boarding school in Aurora. Montgomery meets Ephraim Weber with whom she has corresponded since 1902. The long series of lawsuits against Page ends successfully.

1929   *Magic for Marigold*, featuring a little girl younger than Anne or Emily, is published. Montgomery makes an autumn visit to Prince Edward Island.

1930   Montgomery undertakes a speaking tour through the Canadian West and reestablishes her friendship with Laura Pritchard Agnew.

1931   *A Tangled Web*, the second of her adult novels, is published. Her elder son, Chester, enters the University of

Toronto as an engineering student.

1932   Stuart wins national recognition as a gymnast; Chester fails in his college courses and repeats his first year. Church work involves Montgomery in directing plays for the junior guild. Reunion with Nora Lefurgey Campbell brings healing companionship.

1933   *Pat of Silver Bush* recalls happy Park Corner scenes at the Campbell family home. Stuart enters the University of Toronto as a medical student. Chester fails his second year, withdraws from engineering, and reveals his secret marriage to Luella Reid, the daughter of a church elder.

1934   Ewan spends several months in Homewood, the mental institution in Guelph. He almost dies of accidental poisoning. A first grandchild, Luella, is born to Chester and his wife; Chester is now engaged in the study of law. A second movie is made of *Anne of Green Gables*, still without profit for Montgomery, who had sold all rights for performances to Page. Stock market reverses create financial troubles. Montgomery helps produce a book of biographies, *Courageous Women*. She experiences a six-week breakdown of nerves and general health.

1935   Ill health and misunderstanding in Norval force Ewan to retire from the ministry. The family moves to "Journey's End" in a Humberside suburb of Toronto. *Mistress Pat* is published. Montgomery made a Companion of the Order of the British Empire as part of King George V's jubilee honour list. She is elected to the Literary and Artistic Institute of France.

1936   Stories of Anne as a young teacher appear in *Anne of Windy Poplars*. A second grandchild, Cameron, is born after Luella's return to her family in Norval. The Canadian government designates part of Cavendish a national park, with Green Gables, Lover's Lane, and other spots serving as a shrine to *Anne of Green Gables* for worldwide fans.

1937	A Toronto setting is used for the opening of *Jane of Lantern Hill*. Death of her beloved cat, Good Luck, together with distress over Chester's behaviour, Stuart's romances, and Ewan's severe depression threaten Montgomery's mental health.
1938	Montgomery suffers a nervous collapse but struggles to continue work on her next "Anne" book. Financial problems press: paying Stuart and Chester's university fees, maintaining the Toronto mortgage, and accepting the failure of friends and relations to repay loans made in more affluent times.
1939	Grosset and Dunlap begin reprinting all of Montgomery's early works. She makes her last visit to Prince Edward Island and uses Island scenes in her final work, *Anne of Ingleside*, centred around Anne's happy days of marriage and young motherhood. Montgomery's depression deepens at the outbreak of World War II in September.
1940	Chester is turned down for military service; Stuart is put on the deferred list until his medical training is finished. Montgomery suffers another bout of nervous depression after injuring her arm in a fall. Chester's marriage breaks up. Montgomery works on a final collection of "Anne" stories, later published in 1974 as *The Road to Yesterday*.
1941	Writes her final letter to G.B. Macmillan in December.
1942	L.M. Montgomery dies in Toronto on 24 April 1942 and is buried in Cavendish cemetery, Prince Edward Island, five days later. (Ewan Macdonald dies in 1943.)

WORKS CONSULTED

Åhmansson, Gabriella. *A Life and Its Mirrors: A Feminist Reading of the Work of L.M. Montgomery.* Uppsala, Sweden: U of Uppsala P, 1991.

Atwood, Margaret. Afterword. *Anne of Green Gables.* By L.M. Montgomery. New Canadian Library. Toronto: McClelland, 1992. 331–36.

Bailey, Rosamund. "Little Orphan Mary: Anne's Hoydenish Double." *CCL: Canadian Children's Literature/Littérature canadienne pour la jeunesse* 55 (1989): 8–17.

Bolger, F.W.P. *The Years Before "Anne."* Charlottetown: PEI Heritage Foundation, 1974.

Burns, Jane. "Anne and Emily: L.M. Montgomery's Children." *Room of One's Own* 3.3 (1977): 37–48.

Campbell, Marie. "Wordbound: Women and Language in L.M. Montgomery's *Emily of New Moon* Trilogy." MA Thesis U of Guelph, 1993.

Careless, Virginia. "The Hijacking of 'Anne.'" *CCL: Canadian Children's Literature* 67 (1992): 48–56.

Classen, Constance. "Is 'Anne of Green Gables' an American Import?" *CCL: Canadian Children's Literature* 55 (1989): 42–50.

Coldwell, Joyce-Ione Harrington. "Folklore as Fiction: The Writings of L.M. Montgomery." *Folklore Studies in Honour of Herbert Halpert: A Festschrift.* St. John's: Memorial U of Newfoundland P, 1980. 125–36.

Cowan, Ann S. "Canadian Writers: Lucy Maud & Emily Byrd." *CCL: Canadian Children's Literature* 3 (1975): 42–49.

Drain, Susan. "Feminine Convention and Female Identity: The Persistent Challenge of *Anne of Green Gables.*" *CCL: Canadian Children's Literature* 65 (1992): 40–47.

_____ . "'Too Much Love-Making': *Anne of Green Gables* on Television." *Lion and Unicorn* 11.2 (1987): 63–72.

DuPlessis, Rachel Blau. *Writing Beyond the Ending.* Bloomington: Indiana UP, 1985.

Epperly, Elizabeth Rollins. *The Fragrance of Sweet-Grass: L.M. Montgomery's Heroines and the Pursuit of Romance.* Toronto: U of Toronto P, 1992.

____ . "L.M. Montgomery's *Anne's House of Dreams*: Reworking Poetry." CCL: *Canadian Children's Literature* 37 (1985): 40–46.

Ferns, John. " 'Rainbow Dreams': The Poetry of Lucy Maud Montgomery." CCL: *Canadian Children's Literature* 42 (1986): 29–40.

Fredeman, Jane. "The Land of Lost Content: The Use of Fantasy in L.M. Montgomery's Novels." CCL: *Canadian Children's Literature* 3 (1975): 60–70.

Garner, Barbara, and Mary Harker. "*Anne of Green Gables*: An Annotated Bibliography." CCL: *Canadian Children's Literature* 55 (1989): 18–41.

Gillen, Mollie. *The Wheel of Things: A Biography of L.M. Montgomery.* Toronto: Fitzhenry, 1975.

Katsuro, Yuko. "Red-Haired Anne in Japan." CCL: *Canadian Children's Literature* 34 (1984): 57–60.

Kulyk-Keefer, Janice. *Under Eastern Eyes: A Critical Reading of Maritime Fiction.* Toronto: U of Toronto P, 1987.

Little, Jean. "A Long-Distance Friendship." CCL: *Canadian Children's Literature* 34 (1984): 23–30.

____ . "But What About Jane?" CCL: *Canadian Children's Literature* 3 (1975): 71–82.

MacLulich, T.D. "L.M. Montgomery and the Literary Heroine: Jo, Rebecca, Anne, and Emily." CCL: *Canadian Children's Literature* 37 (1985): 5–17.

McCabe, Kevin. "L.M. Montgomery: The Person and the Poet." CCL: *Canadian Children's Literature* 38 (1985): 68–80.

McGrath, Robin. "*Alice of New Moon*: The Influence of Lewis Carroll on L.M. Montgomery's Emily Bird Starr." CCL: *Canadian Children's Literature* 65 (1992): 62–67.

McMullen, Lorraine, ed. *Re(Dis)covering Our Foremothers.* Ottawa: U of Ottawa P, 1988.

Menzies, Ian. "The Moral of the Rose: L.M. Montgomery's 'Emily.' " CCL: *Canadian Children's Literature* 65 (1992): 48–61.

Montgomery, L.M. *Akin to Anne.* Ed. Rea Wilmshurst. Toronto: McClelland, 1988.

____ . *Along the Shore.* Ed. Rea Wilmshurst. Toronto: McClelland, 1989.

____. *The Alpine Path: The Story of My Career.* 1917. Toronto: Fitzhenry, 1975.

____. *Among the Shadows.* Ed. Rea Wilmshurst. Toronto: McClelland, 1990.

____. *Anne of Avonlea.* Boston: Page, 1909.

____. *Anne of Green Gables.* Boston: Page, 1908.

____. *Anne's House of Dreams.* Toronto: McClelland, 1917.

____. *Anne of Ingleside.* Toronto: McClelland, 1939.

____. *Anne of the Island.* Boston: Page, 1915.

____. *Anne of Windy Poplars.* Toronto: McClelland, 1936.

____. *The Blue Castle.* Toronto: McClelland, 1926.

____. *Chronicles of Avonlea.* Boston: Page, 1912.

____. *The Doctor's Sweetheart and Other Stories.* Ed. Catherine McLay. Toronto: McGraw, 1979.

____. *Emily Climbs.* Toronto: McClelland, 1925.

____. *Emily of New Moon.* Toronto: McClelland, 1923.

____. *Emily's Quest.* Toronto: McClelland, 1925.

____. *Further Chronicles of Avonlea.* Boston: Page, 1920.

____. *The Golden Road.* Boston: Page, 1913.

____. *The Green Gables Letters.* Ed. Wilfrid Eggleston. Toronto: Ryerson, 1960.

____. *Jane of Lantern Hill.* 1937. Toronto: McClelland, 1977.

____. *Kilmeny of the Orchard.* Boston: Page, 1910.

____. *Magic for Marigold.* Toronto: McClelland, 1929.

____. *Mistress Pat: A Novel of Silver Bush.* Toronto: McClelland, 1935.

____. *My Dear Mr. M: Letters to G.B. Macmillan.* Ed. F.W.P. Bolger and Elizabeth Rollins Epperly. Toronto: McGraw, 1980.

____. *Pat of Silver Bush.* Toronto: McClelland, 1933.

____. *The Poetry of Lucy Maud Montgomery.* Ed. John Ferns and Kevin McCabe. Toronto: Fitzhenry, 1987.

____. *Rainbow Valley.* Toronto: McClelland, 1919.

____. *Rilla of Ingleside.* Toronto: McClelland, 1920.

____. *The Road to Yesterday.* Toronto: McGraw, 1974.

____. *The Selected Journals of L.M. Montgomery, Volume I: 1889–1910.* Ed. Mary Rubio and Elizabeth Waterston. Toronto: Oxford UP, 1985. 3 vols. to date.

____. *The Selected Journals of L.M. Montgomery, Volume II: 1910–1921.* Ed. Mary Rubio and Elizabeth Waterston. Toronto: Oxford

UP, 1985. 3 vols. to date.

___ . *The Selected Journals of L.M. Montgomery, Volume III: 1921–1929*. Ed. Mary Rubio and Elizabeth Waterston. Toronto: Oxford UP, 1992. 3 vols. to date.

___ . *The Story Girl*. Boston: Page, 1911.

___ . *A Tangled Web*. Toronto: McClelland, 1931.

___ . Unpublished journals, 1929–42. University of Guelph Archives.

___ . *The Watchman and Other Poems*. Toronto: McClelland, 1916.

Montgomery, L.M., Marian Keith, and M.B. McKinley. *Courageous Women*. Toronto: McClelland, 1934.

Munro, Alice. Afterword. *Emily of New Moon*. By L.M. Montgomery. New Canadian Library. Toronto: McClelland, 1989. 357–61.

Mustard, Margaret. *L.M. Montgomery as Mrs. Ewan Macdonald of the Leaskdale Manse: 1911–1926*. Leaskdale, ON: St. Paul's Presbyterian Women's Association, 1964.

Pratt, Annis. *Archetypal Patterns in Women's Fiction*. Bloomington: Indiana UP, 1981.

Reimer, Mavis, ed. *Such a Simple Little Tale: Critical Responses to L.M. Montgomery's* Anne of Green Gables. Metuchen, NJ: Children's Literature Association, 1991.

Rubio, Jennie. " 'In an Alphabet I Did Not Know': Reading Space in Montgomery, Laurence and Munro." MA Thesis McMaster U, 1992.

Rubio, Mary Henley. " 'Anne of Green Gables': Architect of Adolescence." *Touchstones: Reflections on the Best in Children's Literature*. Ed. Perry Nodelman. Vol. 1. West Lafayette, IN: Children's Literature Association, 1985. 173–87. 3 vols. 1985–89.

___ , ed. *Harvesting Thistles: The Textual Garden of L.M. Montgomery: Essays on Her Novels and Journals*. Guelph: Canadian Children's Press, 1994.

___ . "L.M. Montgomery: Where Does the Voice Come From?" *Canadiana: Studies in Canadian Literature*. Proc. of the University of Aarhus Canadian Studies Conference. 1984. Ed. Jørn Carlsen and Knud Larsen. Aarhus, Denmark: Dept. of English, 1984. 109–19.

___ . "Lucy Maud Montgomery." *Profiles in Canadian Literature: 7*. Ed. Jeffrey M. Heath. Toronto: Dundurn, 1991. 37–45. 7 vols. 1980–91.

____ . "Satire, Realism and Imagination in *Anne of Green Gables*." CCL: *Canadian Children's Literature* 3 (1975): 27–36.

____ . "Subverting the Trite: L.M. Montgomery's Room of Her Own." CCL: *Canadian Children's Literature* 65 (1992): 6–39.

Rubio, Mary, and Elizabeth Waterston. Afterword. *Anne of Avonlea*. By L.M. Montgomery. Signet Classics Series. New York: Penguin, 1987. 274–85.

____ . Afterword. *Anne of Green Gables*. By L.M. Montgomery. Signet Classics Series. New York: Penguin, 1987. 307–17.

____ . Afterword. *Anne of the Island*. By L.M. Montgomery. Signet Classics Series. New York: Penguin, 1990. 239–48.

____ . Afterword. *Anne's House of Dreams*. By L.M. Montgomery. Signet Classics Series. New York: Penguin, 1991. 277–86.

____ . Afterword. *Chronicles of Avonlea*. By L.M. Montgomery. Signet Classics Series. New York: Penguin, 1988. 238–51.

____ . Afterword. *The Story Girl*. By L.M. Montgomery. Signet Classics Series. New York: Penguin, 1991. 277–88.

Russell, R.W., D.W. Russell, and Rea Wilmshurst. *Lucy Maud Montgomery: A Preliminary Bibliography*. Waterloo: U of Waterloo Library, 1986.

Smith, Sidonie. *A Poetics of Women's Autobiography*. Bloomington: Indiana UP, 1987.

Sobkowska, Krystyna. "The Reception of the *Anne of Green Gables* Series by Lucy Maud Montgomery in Poland." MA Thesis U of Lodz, Poland, 1982–83.

Sorfleet, John R., ed. *L.M. Montgomery: An Assessment*. Guelph: Canadian Children's Press, 1976.

Tausky, Thomas E. "L.M. Montgomery and 'The Alpine Path, So Hard, So Steep.'" CCL: *Canadian Children's Literature* 30 (1985): 5–20.

Thomas, Gillian. "The Decline of Anne: Matron vs. Child." CCL: *Canadian Children's Literature* 3 (1975): 37–41.

Trollope, Anthony. *Small House at Allington*. 1864. World Classic Series. Oxford: Oxford UP, 1980.

Urquhart, Jane. Afterword. *Emily Climbs*. By L.M. Montgomery. New Canadian Library. Toronto: McClelland, 1989. 330–34.

Wachowicz, Barbara. "L.M. Montgomery: At Home in Poland." CCL: *Canadian Children's Literature* 46 (1987): 7–36.

Waterston, Elizabeth. *Children's Literature in Canada*. New York: Twayne, 1992.

___ . *"Kindling Spirit"*: *Lucy Maud Montgomery's* Anne of Green Gables. Canadian Fiction Studies 19. Toronto: ECW, 1993.

___ . "Lucy Maud Montgomery." *The Clear Spirit: Twenty Canadian Women and Their Times*. Ed. Mary Quayle Innis. Toronto: U of Toronto P, 1966. 198–220.

___ . "Women in Canadian Fiction." *Canadiana: Studies in Canadian Literature*. Proc. of the University of Aarhus Canadian Studies Conference. 1984. Ed. Jørn Carlsen and Knud Larsen. Aarhus, Denmark: Dept. of English, 1984. 100–08.

Whitaker, Muriel A. " 'Queer Children:' L.M. Montgomery's Heroines." CCL: *Canadian Children's Literature* 3 (1975): 50–59.

Wiggins, Genevieve. *L.M. Montgomery*. Twayne's World Authors Series. New York: Macmillan, 1992.

Wilmshurst, Rea. "L.M. Montgomery's Short Stories: A Preliminary Bibliography." CCL: *Canadian Children's Literature* 29 (1983): 25–34.

___ . "L.M. Montgomery's Use of Quotations and Allusions in the 'Anne' Books." CCL: *Canadian Children's Literature* 56 (1989): 15–45.

Yeast, Denyse Elaine. "Negotiating and Articulating a Self: An Intertextual Reading of L.M. Montgomery's Public and Private Writings." MA Thesis U of Calgary, 1993.